SIDEWALKS VOLUME II

SIDEWALKS _{VOLUME} II

REFLECTIONS ON CHICAGO

RICK KOGAN

PHOTOGRAPHS BY
CHARLES OSGOOD

SIDEWALKS
BOOK COMPANY

Sidewalks Book Company
www.sidewalksbookcompany.com

Printed in China

10 9 8 7 6 5 4 3 2 1

ISBN 978-0-9841265-0-7

Page ii: Six corners, Wicker Park
Page v: Mayor Spookenburger (Jeff Jenkins, Midnight Circus) performs,
    Mayor Richard M. Daley watches, Daley Plaza
Page vi: A Sunday Afternoon on the Island of La Grande Jatte,
    Art Institute of Chicago
Page viii: Fork in the walk, Evanston
Page x: Gold Coast dog
Page 242: Logan Square, dusk
Page 246: Lunar eclipse, Marina City

Library of Congress Control Number: 2009906443

This book is printed on acid-free paper.

Book design by Kim Bartko

FOR VIA AND ZAC
FOR FIONA

PREFACE

It began on a sultry summer day more than a decade ago, when Charles Osgood grabbed his camera (actually a couple of cameras) and I grabbed a notebook and pen and we left the Tribune Tower in search of stories. We have found hundreds, discovering them in the most unlikely and sometimes forlorn places.

Some of these (113 to be exact) were collected in a handsome book, *Sidewalks: Portraits of Chicago*, published by Northwestern University Press in 2006.

This second book was born of the response we received to the first book. As we visited dozens of libraries, schools, and other places to talk about the book and the column, we began to realize that Sidewalks struck a nerve, or nerves. Sometimes a column evoked memories, sometimes it introduced people to a new restaurant or gallery or adventure, or to a part of the past almost forgotten.

"It's about ordinary people," we were told again and again.

The people in this book are not famous (okay, Bill Murray and Studs Terkel make appearances). The people in this book are not newsmakers. But they are doing something equally, if not more, important. They are making life.

And there is nothing ordinary about them. They are, and it's true of all of us, if we take the time to listen, extraordinary. And so, you will be introduced to a ghost or two, visit oases of hope and courage, and get to know a man who artfully painted his face every day for a year. The people in this book are, though you have never met them, your neighbors, sharing this remarkable place and time.

I have been a newspaperman my whole life and yet it has taken Sidewalks to remind me that certain quiet stories are as important as those below blaring headlines.

Here is a gathering of life as people live it. In Osgood's photos (and yes, my words) we hope you will find what Chicago is and discover clues to what it may yet become.

As in the first book, I have chosen here not to update any of the entries. The dates you will see on the pages are the dates the stories ran in the *Chicago Tribune Magazine*. Discover them as we did and enjoy the attendant surprise.

You will find nine longer pieces here that have no dates. These are stories that combine Sidewalks columns with some other writing done for the newspaper. It just did not seem right, and would have been nightmarish, to try to squeeze the large lives of Studs or Leon Despres, and the rich lives of taverns or Maxwell Street, into five hundred or so words.

Some of the people and places in this book have vanished—dead or razed. This is not news. I have known for a long time that people and places come and go. I know too that their stories remain, to help and to haunt, and even inspire.

SIDEWALKS VOLUME II

FIGHTING FOR A FRESH START

Most of those in the largely male crowd of a couple hundred were standing. More than a few were drinking. A surprising number were smoking. A few were filled with bloodthirsty expectation. "Let's get it on!" screamed one crew-cut man to no one in particular. "Let's see some action." He was downstairs in one of the cavernous rooms of the sprawling entertainment complex known as 115 Bourbon Street, at 3359 West 115th Street in south suburban Merrionette Park. He and the others were awaiting a series of boxing matches to be held in the regulation-size ring that towered over the floor, illuminated by almost blindingly bright lights.

In a large room upstairs (as seen in Osgood's photo), there was plenty of action as young men, teenagers, really, shadowboxed, skipped rope, and otherwise prepared for their bouts under the concerned eyes and whispered counsel of parents, coaches, or trainers.

You may not realize it, but boxing matches are a frequent and popular diversion around the area. They take place regularly in gymnasiums and in such larger venues as the Aragon, Cicero Stadium in Cicero, Sabre Room, and 115 Bourbon Street, where you can see for yourself on the third Wednesday of every month.

You might meet Martin McGarry, who, when not working as a union pipe fitter for Local 597, runs McGarry's Boxing Club on the Far South Side.

"The boxing scene here is very healthy," said McGarry, a native of Ireland and, when he was younger, an accomplished boxer there and in England. "More people are getting involved. There are some very good amateur fighters here. Some of the kids in this room, maybe a few of them, have thoughts of turning professional one day. But a lot do it for exercise, or to learn how to protect themselves."

The proceeds from the boxing matches on this night will benefit the First Chance Program of the Police Athletic League of Illinois (www.illinoiscrimecommission.com). Jerry Elsner, director of PAL and executive director of the Illinois State Crime Commission, was standing ringside.

"Look, a kid can get in trouble a lot of ways," he said. "Let's say he's at a party where the police find dope, or he's busted at a party for underage drinking. Well, that goes on his record, and—this is the computer age—it stays there. But a kid gets in our program and does what he needs to, the charges will be dropped."

McGarry said: "This is a great program. A lot of kids get jammed up on something innocent. This enables them to get back on the right track. A lot of these at-risk kids get involved in boxing programs. But what I tell my kids is that they don't have to fight competitively to gain great self-esteem and confidence…to get on the right track, to have a good life."

APRIL 8, 2007

HEART STRINGS

No easy job, tuning a harp, or at least that's the way it appears in Osgood's photo. No easy job, getting respect for one either. This bulky but beautiful instrument, ancient in its roots, has made its way onto the soundtracks of some enlightened or adventurous jazz and rock musicians, but it remains relatively unappreciated by anything approaching masses. You are unlikely to have a harp tune in your iPod, but have you ever even heard one?

I have, and still will, when the opportunity presents itself. This attraction began many years ago when I walked into a dark wood/thick curtains/chandeliers/oil portraits place called the Royal Garden Cocktail Lounge in what was then the Ambassador West Hotel. Sitting there, as she had for most evenings during the previous six years, was a regal-looking woman (the long black formal gown helped) plucking the strings of an ornate harp to surprising effect: People were actually listening.

These people, most of them conventioneer types awaiting the dubious pleasures (which then included a couple of what were charmingly called "nudie joints") a few blocks south on Rush Street, seemed genuinely taken with the playing of Doriss Briggs. She gave them a full dose of the versatility of her harp with an eclectic selection that included "What I Did for Love," "To All the Girls I've Loved Before," "On the Road Again," and "City of New Orleans."

"People are always surprised by what the harp can do," Briggs said between sets. She also told me about a group of conventioneers from a few nights before who, well-lubricated, had bets against one another about whether she (and her harp) could play "Dixie." To their amazed pleasure, she did.

She was one of the city's musical treasures. Classically trained, she had played with the Chicago Symphony Orchestra, and she played a lot of private parties and had some TV commercials to her credit. She had also shared a stage, at various times, with such performers as Frank Sinatra, Judy Garland, and Tony Bennett. Her harp, she told me, had forty-nine strings, seven foot pedals and, she added proudly, "fifteen hundred moving parts."

I neglected then to ask who had made it, but it likely came from the craftsmen at Lyon & Healy, the local firm that had built its first harp here in 1889.

Those of you who might have thought the company ceased to exist when it moved from its prominent Wabash Avenue home in the Loop in the early 1980s (music under the "L") will be pleased to know that Lyon & Healy is still going strong here, with offices, factory, and showroom at 168 North Ogden Avenue. That is where Osgood took the photo of harpist Nuiko Wadden earlier this year. She was preparing for one of the many concerts held in the building's handsome Lyon & Healy Hall. The next will feature harpists Elizabeth Hainen and Angel Padilla Crespo.

I have never heard either, but it has been written of the latter that his "trills are unlike those of any other harpist in the world," and that's good enough for me.

OCTOBER 26, 2008

THE HELPFUL PLACE

You cannot tell the history of a neighborhood by its commercial streets. Though buildings may hint at bygone purposes, at street level the storefronts are mostly the come-and-go kind. And so, on Seventy-eighth Street, you see fast-food shops and nail emporiums and barbershops of such obviously recent vintage that most might as well have opened yesterday. Then in the middle of one block you spot a store that appears as though it might have been there forever, or at least for a very long while. That feeling is confirmed when you walk into R.H. Sneed, 1650 West Seventy-eighth Street, and find yourself transported back in time. Sneed's is to the massive, lavishly stocked, and seductively arranged megastores in the suburbs or in more well-heeled neighborhoods what your nearby park's baseball diamond is to Wrigley Field. It's a tiny place where the merchandise, which includes jars filled with various seeds for backyard planting, seems randomly arranged, though the employees can in an instant direct you to whatever you need.

But if you are looking for a variety of colorful porch umbrellas, or 125 snazzy hammers or drills, you'll have to go elsewhere. This is a place that meets basic needs; where, one recent Saturday, one man wanted ten nails, another bought a mop, and a woman purchased a pair of knives.

The store is owned by Ramon Harris, standing front and center in Osgood's photo. That's his daughter/partner Yolanda Harris behind him, and employees Steven and Carl Clay.

Yolanda, who works full time for Bank of America, is proud of the store's longevity. It has been here since 1968, the second of two hardware stores once owned and operated by William Sneed, who, she says, was "one of the first African-American hardware-store owners in the city."

Her father became owner of the store more than twenty years ago, after having worked at Sneed's stores since he was a teenager. "Mr. Sneed was more than an employer to him; he was a friend, mentor, and father figure. My dad called him Papa," Yolanda says.

The Harrises have long hired people who have, Yolanda says—perhaps putting it mildly— "led wayward lives." The store has partnerships with James Simmons, a minister and general contractor, and Gerald Manuel, a pastor and engineer who specializes in electrical work and plumbing. "They further assist the men with mentoring and spiritual guidance, teaching them how to apply the knowledge they learn here to practical situations," she says. "This is a grass-roots solution to tackling some of the problems that are prevalent in the area. They are being taught the hardware business, literally learning the nuts and bolts necessary to build rather than tear down a community."

NOVEMBER 16, 2008

MAN IN THE SKY

"I call him the Giant Man," said a little boy named Steve, walking with some of his buddies along the 3900 block of West Grand Avenue late one afternoon. "And I call him the Monster Man," said another in this crowd of kids. There were six of them, who, as Steve said, were all eight years old "except Billy, who's nine." And Billy said, "I call him the Giant Man too." He is something of a neighborhood curiosity, the Giant/Monster Man that stands atop a place called CEDS–Interstate Muffler Brake & Spring Service. The statue looked to me like someone's vision of mythical lumberjack Paul Bunyan. Osgood thought it resembled Abraham Lincoln.

Everyone we talked to on the street expressed a fondness for the statue, and some, mostly kids, had a name for it, even though a close look tells you the figure already has a name. He is "Mr. Bendo," as indicated by the lettering above the pocket of his shirt.

And who is that?

"The man who used to own this place," said Frank Shalabi, the manager of Interstate. "They tell me he looked a lot like the statue, with the beard and everything."

This is a city filled with statues. Most of them are of familiar figures, such as Lincoln and Ulysses S. Grant, Christopher Columbus and William Shakespeare. There are a few statues of relatively obscure but important figures, such as Karel Havlicek, the Czech patriot, who has a statue near the Adler Planetarium, and John Alexander Logan, the Civil War general, congressman, and creator of Memorial Day, whose statue is in Grant Park. The Tin Man of *Wizard of Oz* renown has a statue in, fittingly, Oz Park.

No one seems to know who made Mr. Bendo, or even how long he has been on the roof. "A long time," said Shalabi. "It reminds me of the huge Indian statue on a building on the South Side near where I used to live."

Mr. Bendo is secured to the roof by wires, and his right arm is outstretched. In his hand there is a piece of metal, from which a sign used to hang.

"I think it looks like some kind of thing that you would hit people with," said Steve, and his pals seemed to agree.

"But I don't think he's a mean guy," said Billy.

An icy wind blew down the sidewalk, and one of the boys wondered, "Do statues get cold?"

DECEMBER 3, 2000

THE NATURAL

This column was written on the bone-chillingly cold morning preceding the Cubs' 2007 home opener and was finished before anyone knew the score of the game, its heroes, and its goats. But the start of every season, filled with usually misguided hopes for the future, is actually a time of involuntary reflection as the mind fills with images of seasons past, memories that often come in black and white. And so, here in my head this morning is Jim Brosnan.

He was, if you are too young or too old to remember, a pitcher. He played for the Cubs (1954, 1956–58) and the White Sox (1963), though his best year came in 1961, when he helped the Cincinnati Reds win the National League pennant with a 10–4 record and 16 saves.

By then, however, he was more famous as the author of a book, *The Long Season*. It was a diary of the 1959 campaign, when Brosnan was with the St. Louis Cardinals and the Reds. It was revolutionary, taking fans behind the scenes—from clubhouses to hotel rooms, dugouts to airplanes—with an intimacy that had never before been available on the sports pages.

Reviewing the book for the *New York Herald Tribune*, the great sportswriter Red Smith called it, "An honest book that furnished an insight into the ballplayer's life which no outsider could possibly get…a cocky book, caustic and candid and, in a way, courageous, for Brosnan calls them as he sees them, doesn't hesitate to name names, and employs ridicule like a stiletto."

Brosnan would play for three more seasons, compiling a lifetime record of 55–47 with 67 saves, and then devote himself full-time to writing. He and his wife, Anne, had bought a modest north suburban home when he was with the Cubs, and in his basement office he has turned out hundreds of magazine articles, book reviews, essays, instructional books, and biographies, including one of Ron Santo.

Nothing he would write would match *The Long Season*. In the world of words, it was his perfect game.

Pulitzer Prize-winning book critic Jonathan Yardley, in a 2004 rereview of the book in the *Washington Post,* wrote that it "not merely changed everything, it remains, decades later, the best of its kind."

Originally published by Harper, the book is now available, appropriately, through local publisher Ivan R. Dee. Depending on your age, you might not recognize many of the players, but you will know the game and see it in ways that remain humorous, enlightening and, yes, fresh.

The last time I saw Brosnan, he and his wife were in a suburban bookstore, looking for something to read.

He has recently been beset by health problems (he is closing in on eighty), but he was upbeat. So, on this Opening Day, my mind runs to Jim Brosnan and the realization that *The Long Season* and its author will be remembered and cheered long after this season is in the books.

APRIL 29, 2007

THE STREET OF SARIS

Show me a more interesting Chicago street than Devon Avenue. Traveling its length is, in essence, a unique experience of sights and sounds, like a trip around the world. The shops cluster together, a panorama of different ethnic goods, foods, and services. Whenever Osgood and I get depressed by some new ticky-tacky townhouse complex, or the appearance of yet another Starbucks, we take a trip to this street.

We are not looking for anything specific, just eager to walk around, for we know that we will be reminded of the glorious diversity of the city and of its ability to be hospitable to almost anyone who wants to stake a claim. This is a street, 6400 north for those of you who don't venture out much, that pleasantly assaults the eye and the other senses with a wild mix of signs and styles and faces. A friend of ours once said, "Devon looks like the back lot of some movie studio, with a million extras wandering around."

Among the most visually stimulating sights here are the sari shops, most of which are spaced along a few blocks on either side of Western Avenue. The oldest of them have been here since the mid-1970s, when Indians and Pakistanis began moving to the neighborhood in significant numbers. In any given year since, between fifteen and twenty sari stores have coexisted on a strip that is less than a mile in length.

There is almost no comparable concentration of similar businesses in the city, except perhaps for the saloons crowding Division and Rush Streets, or the financial institutions on LaSalle Street.

To the untrained eye—and Osgood and I are far from knowledgeable about fashion—the stores appear little different from one another.

Their windows are alive with brightly colored fabrics, some with intricate designs full of meaning—reflecting, for instance, the changing seasons.

The sari is many centuries old and is, basically, a six- or seven-yard piece of fabric that is draped artfully—with the aid of pleating and tucks, and over a drawstring underskirt and blouse—on the body to make the most elegant of outfits.

"There are basically two kinds of saris," says Manohar Thadani, who with his wife, Shreen, has operated Sari Sapne, 2623 West Devon Avenue, since 1986. "Ones made of silk and embroidered are generally worn for fancy or formal occasions. "Others are made of polyester imported from Japan. These less-expensive polyester saris are not available in India, so many are bought here by people who are going back to India to visit relatives. In India, the sari is everyday wear."

The saris at Sari Sapne are in the ten- to four hundred-dollar range, but other stores have prices of one thousand dollars and more. It's a competitive market. "Very competitive during the day," says Thadani. "But at night we get together and have a party."

SEPTEMBER 19, 1999

FROM THE GROUND UP

There is a great tavern in Three Oaks, Michigan, called the Nelson Saloon, and one Friday night a few weeks ago, the drinks flowed and conversations filled the air. Some tables were filled with locals, while others contained some of the many, many people who have summer homes in this area, commonly known as Harbor Country and conveniently little more than an hour from Chicago.

One ever-expanding table was filled with a few locals and more than a dozen people who had just come from a show at the Acorn Theater, one of the most adventurous arts/entertainment performance venues in the country.

The men who own, run, and live in the Acorn bought the place, a run-down factory, in 2001 with modest intentions. That's them in Osgood's photo. On the left is David Fink, who some years ago quit his job as president of a manufacturing company to devote himself to the arts. The other man is Kim Clark, a director and playwright who teaches screenwriting at DePaul University and ran unsuccessfully in 2006 for the House seat from Michigan's Sixth Congressional District. (It was an uphill battle to be sure, since no Democrat has held that spot since Franklin Roosevelt was president.) The dog is their vivacious sheltie, Emes.

"We never really thought of having anything more than a black box space for our friends," says Clark. "But things just started growing."

"It wasn't too long before we began to see it as part theater, part arts incubator, and part community center," says Fink. "Still, you never know how things will work out."

They have succeeded beyond all dreams and reason, offering, and drawing crowds for, as satisfyingly eclectic a stream of acts as you are likely to find, from opera to jazz, Jefferson Starship to flamenco to bluegrass.

"There really isn't anything we won't try," says Fink.

"At least once," says Clark.

On the recent Friday night at Nelson's, they sat with authors (including me) who had been part of an onstage conversation on the topics of crime, punishment, and justice, the first in what Fink and Clark hope will be a series of literary salons. I can speak for all the participants in saying we had a blast. But writers are so easily pleased. Let's hear from musical performers, a pickier bunch.

Alan Barcus, the composer-pianist-singer from nearly LaPorte, Indiana, says: "The Acorn Theater is a venue that would seem right at home in any major city in the country....Surviving the early stages of booking acts into a very small Michigan town had to be extremely difficult, but they persevered, and the results have been amazing. I promised myself I would never again use the now-devalued word 'amazing,' but nothing else seems appropriate."

NOVEMBER 2, 2008

TANKS FOR THE MEMORIES

They keep building skyscrapers in this skyscraper town, and so many of them do little to brighten the view. If you don't believe us, read *Chicago Tribune* architecture critic Blair Kamin's assessments of the scene. Earlier this year he wrote about the "rogues gallery of condominium and apartment towers, all either new or completed in the last few years... structures that offend not only because they're poorly designed but also because they erode the city's extraordinary sense of place."

As the city fills with these new loud towers, it continues to lose its quiet little gems. That's one of them in Osgood's photo, and there are more—thirty-seven, to be exact—in photos and reproductions of paintings in Larry Green's charming and important book, *Water Tanks of Chicago: A Vanishing Urban Legacy*. It is the first book from Wicker Park Press, the creation of Eric Lincoln Miller, who is determined to publish a stream of books about Chicago landmarks; the next one is about the bygone Maxwell Street market.

Green, an Indiana native who came here to study at the School of the Art Institute in 1971 and never left, is passionate about the tanks, writing, "They are a fascinating part of Chicago's history and one of the city's unique architectural landmarks."

Though he can get a bit rhapsodic ("You see them overlooking, with silent observation, life in the metropolis"), his ardor is justified. These water tanks are nestled among the city like so many hidden jewels. Some might disagree, but we think it's a wise choice Green made to not give us the location of the tanks. This way they are allowed to come at us as visual surprises. It took us only a few minutes of driving around the Near Northwest Side to find six of them. Just look!

They were built in the wake of the Great Chicago Fire of 1871—made of redwood, fir, and cypress, and later metal—atop apartment and commercial buildings to guarantee a supply of water in case of fire and for use in some manufacturing tasks. Inevitably, they began to vanish, their number shrinking from nearly a thousand to about 120 still used today.

In 2005, an exhibition was mounted to remind us of the tanks. It was sponsored by the city and the Chicago Architectural Club, and came in the form of a competition to identify new uses for the tanks. Among the 182 entries from nineteen countries: transforming them into energy-producing wind turbines, huge beehives, and giant planters; painting them in the images of such local icons as Mike Ditka and Mrs. O'Leary's cow; turning them into campgrounds or art studios.

At the time, Jim Peters, director of planning for the Landmarks Preservation Council of Illinois, said, "Church steeples and water tanks in most neighborhoods are the icons of the skyline."

But let Green have the last word, and consider it a call to buy his book and to just look: "They have not yet gone the way of the dinosaurs, but they are nearing the point of extinction."

MARCH 16, 2008

ROSTER CHANGE

One day years from now, when she is walking and talking and exploring her little world, Macy Dale McMichael will have a lot of questions for her parents. It is normal for kids to have a lot of questions for their parents, but Macy's are likely to be unusual. "How many broken bones do you have, Daddy?" Daddy is Steve McMichael, the former Chicago Bear. Mommy is named Misty.

"Sleeping, not sleeping, pooping, it's all wonderful," says the mother.

When Osgood and I visited them a few weeks ago in their cramped, one-bedroom apartment near the north edge of Lincoln Park, they were happy as happy can be.

"The greatest thing that ever happened to me," says the father, owner of a Super Bowl ring from 1986. "It just killed us at first, and it just gets better every day."

A baby is something the couple wanted ever since they married in 2000, a couple of Texas-tough, rough-and-tumble characters coming off marriages that worked out badly.

Macy Dale was born January 22 (6 pounds 12 ounces, 19 inches for statistics freaks). McMichael's mother, a lively septuagenarian named Betty Lou, was there. So was Misty's mom. Jim and Nancy McMahon, too; the former quarterback and McMichael teammate and his wife are parents of four kids.

"They were all so happy, but no one was happier than we were," says Misty. The field includes some of the nurses and doctors who asked for and got autographed photos of the father.

In the wake of Macy's birth, the family's apartment began to fill with gifts from friends and fans, and you can just imagine the theme: bears, bears, and more bears, dressed in or emblazoned with Bears colors and logos. Macy often wears tiny Bears clothing, or that of the Chicago Slaughter of the Continental Indoor Football League, a team her father coaches, in addition to his ESPN radio work and a busy personal-appearance schedule.

"We want to be the best parents," says Misty. "We've had some wild times in the past, but now everything we do we will be doing for our little girl. That's the most important thing in our lives."

They are adjusting, eagerly, to the demands and responsibilities of parenthood. Their Chihuahua named Chula, previously the baby of the household, has adjusted, too.

"Chula likes Macy," says the father. "And my little girl is getting so big. It wasn't so long ago that I could hold her, all of her, in my hand."

Being a parent is not an easy task. Like all parents, Steve and Misty wish they could hold their kid in their hands forever. It's a tough world out there, but it might go a bit easier for Macy, who, one day years from now, will be able to tell some schoolyard bully, "Don't do that or my daddy will get you, and he's a Bear."

MAY 25, 2008

MOTHERING NATURE

A coyote prowls Lincoln Park. It wanders around Cardinal Francis George's house in the Gold Coast. For a couple of days, worlds collide and we city folk are reminded that, for all of our parks, pigeons, zoos, and green initiatives, we live far, far removed from nature. So, it is important to get in a car (yes, there is irony in that) and go where the eyes can no longer see skyscrapers, and where a coyote does not make front-page news (or appear on the *Chicago Tribune* Web site in a twenty-six-second video shot by, of all people, Osgood).

In so doing, you might find yourself near Baraboo. This is a Wisconsin town of about twelve thousand people, two hundred or so miles from Chicago, north of the state capital of Madison, and

near the water-logged playground that is the Wisconsin Dells. It is home to such amusements as the Circus World Museum and Ho-Chunk Hotel and Casino. It is a pleasant locale, and five miles north you will find a special place called the International Crane Foundation. It was started in 1973 by a couple of young ornithologists named George Archibald and Ron Sauey on the horse farm owned by Sauey's parents.

Those were desperate times: Across the world, cranes were increasingly endangered, and these two guys and some volunteers wanted to preserve and restore wetlands and grasslands, the cranes' natural habitats, and thereby facilitate the breeding of these beautiful birds. They started with twelve of them. (The collection of creatures at Lincoln Park Zoo, it might be noted for those staying in town, began with two swans that arrived here by train in 1869, a gift from New York City's Central Park.)

The crane foundation long ago moved to bigger digs—225 acres of prairie and savanna and marsh—and is now home to all fifteen of the world's crane species. Here you will find Demoiselle cranes (the name means "young lady" in French) and red-eyed sarus cranes, the tallest flying birds in the world, stretching to six feet. You will see South African blue cranes, with their saber-like beaks.

You will see the most famous of the flock, the whooping cranes. In the 1940s, it was estimated that there were only fifteen such birds on the planet. Now, thanks in large part to the efforts of the International Crane Foundation, there are more than 650. The tiny one in Osgood's photo is being fed by a camouflaged attendant to minimize human contact and allow the birds to retain their wildness.

As you read this, know that these little birds have grown and been introduced to mature cranes with which they will, when the weather turns, migrate south. Though some of the cranes born at the foundation will remain there for life, most are released into the wild, here and in other countries. None, as far as we know, has settled in a city.

AUGUST 19, 2007

A RIVER RUNS THROUGH IT

Any sunny summer day, and some not so sunny, the river is filled with boats. They come in all shapes and sizes and are filled with gawking tourists, beer-swilling frat boys, serious sailors, sunbathers…all manner of people drawn for all manner of reasons to our wet and matchless urban road. It is a very fine river.

It is not the Thames or the Seine or the Tiber, but it is not without its charms and its interesting history. It was, for a couple of centuries after its discovery by French explorers, a much-maligned waterway. It was once called the River of Onions, for the foul smell it produced.

And some time later, when the stockyards were in full and bloody operation, a portion of the river was called Bubbly Creek, for it was filled with animal carcasses and waste that would bubble to the surface.

In 1900, in a masterful piece of engineering, the river's flow was reversed. But it still has, as always, three branches and is some fifty miles in total length.

It has one island (Goose Island) and an estimated twenty-five species of fish. It is twenty-one feet at its deepest point and eight hundred feet at its widest.

Portions of two golf courses hug its shoreline (Edgebrook and Billy Caldwell), and two cemeteries (St. Luke and Bohemian National). And every summer, it seems, a new cafe or restaurant opens offering intimate, watery views.

The newest boat on the Chicago River is the largest in the Wendella fleet and one of the largest on the river, a ninety-foot-long, thirty-foot-wide beauty able to seat nearly 350 people. Construction began in March 2006 in Rhode Island. The boat was christened there on May 16, 2007 and, after a trip through rivers, canals, and Great Lakes, made its Chicago appearance on June 21.

"And a good thing too, because we had a wedding booked for the twenty-third," says Bob Borgstrom, the CEO of Wendella Sightseeing Boats. "That's the reason we had the boat built. We had been missing out on big events like weddings and parties. It's gotten so fiercely competitive. There used to be just a few boats, a couple of companies, and now…"

Borgstrom is the river. It has been part of his life and he part of it since he was fourteen years old and began working for his father, Albert, who started the Wendella line in 1935 with a ninety-seven-foot wooden boat operating from Navy Pier.

The boat moved to the river a few years later, and in 1962 Wendella inaugurated its successful and enduring commuter service between the train stations near Madison Street and the Michigan Avenue Bridge.

Though Bob remains the head of the company and comes downtown a couple of days a week, its day-to-day operations are in the hands of his two sons, Steve and Mike, who, when not working, can often be heard at various street fairs and bars playing in their band, the Captain Blood Orchestra (Steve on guitar, Mike on drums).

To sit with Bob Borgstrom, which can happen in the Billy Goat Tavern (he claims, and no one disputes the point, to have been the first customer when the saloon's subterranean Hubbard Street location opened in 1964), is to be wildly entertained, but also to be transported through time.

He will, of course, talk about his wife, Lila, whom he has known and loved since they were teenagers, his sons, and his four granddaughters. And the river, always the river. "Forty years ago, the river was ugly, filthy," he says. "Now you see the banks alive with trees, small parks. There are geese, ducks. It's so alive."

"I'll be seventy-four in September, and I gave up captaining a couple of years ago. Hell, I'd been doing it for more than fifty years. But I'm renewing my captain's license. Got to do that every five years, and this will be my eleventh. I can't give up the river just yet."

He's lucky that way. No matter how worldly we like to feel, we all live in our own little worlds, savvy only about our particular portions of the larger sphere. For most of us, and I include those who live in the vastness of suburbia and nearby states, the Chicago River and Lake Michigan are glorious and important part of our worlds.

The lake defines our place on this planet and has always been a powerful magnet. To the Indian tribes here forever, it was life. Settlers went there to drink and to bathe. It sheltered those fleeing the Great Fire of 1871 and was, for a time before air conditioners, where entire families spent summer nights. You almost certainly have been in the lake, or done a season of sunbathing, swimming, bodybuilding, jogging, skating, running, Frisbee tossing, volleyball playing, bicycling, fishing, or any of the other activities that invigorate our twenty-nine miles of lakefront with its thirty-two city beaches.

But not all are as fortunate.

Tom Castle has met them. He is a sailor, musical performer, and historian of, and an advocate for, the Great Lakes. "I was doing a residency with the Friends of the Chicago River a few years back and found that over half of our audience of about four hundred students at a school near the North Branch of the Chicago River did not know where the Chicago River was," he says. "Also, while doing a summer reading program concert series at more than forty libraries, I found, through an informal raising of hands, that anywhere from 10 to 80 percent of the people in the audiences had never seen Lake Michigan."

Of course, you can blame these people or their parents. Our beaches are free (along the miles of lakefront north of the city, twenty-six of the beaches are private). The river runs, no admission.

But for reasons disturbing to ponder, many people are deprived of the waters. Castle was shocked by this, and it became what he calls "a key catalyst for establishing the outreach program for the Chicago Maritime Festival," an annual event he helps organize.

The lake makes it possible to be in the city but be apart from it, to turn away from its bustle and sit on the shore. There you realize that what you are seeing is exactly what someone saw a hundred or a thousand years ago: the waters of an ancient lake seemingly unalterable. It is a calming sight, but it is impossible not to eventually be interrupted by, not to wonder and worry about, the city behind you.

If, in some fantastical flight of time, you were able to turn around and find the city, in an instant, one hundred years older, what would you see? Which of the forces so energetically at play this year will have triumphed, or will the battle still be raging? It is likely to be a city built on a series of miracles and mistakes, a combination of the wicked and the wonderful. But it is hoped that it will be, as it is now, for better and for worse, a city certifiably alive.

Many years ago Osgood and I met a seven-year-old girl who lived in the Robert Taylor Homes and had never seen a tree. This haunts us still, with its painful perspective.

Before this, when I stood at the shore, turning my back on the city and being transported back in time looking at the ten-thousand-year-old lake, it was, given the stress and troubles and inequities that are part of city life, a reassuring sight. Knowing that there are those living here who have never had this view, it is no longer such a comfort.

INSIDE BASEBALL

In an otherwise ordinary-looking condo in Buffalo Grove, an extraordinary man is completing a stunning replica of Boston's Fenway Park. What Steve Wolf does, often up to sixteen hours a day, is not the kind of thing most of us understand. It is a solitary pursuit, an almost painfully meticulous process, an endeavor that might cause some to think of Wolf as an oddball. He's not nuts. "I love what I'm doing," he says. "It's a passion."

He will tell you that on September 30, 1990, he cried while watching the last game played in old Comiskey Park. This sorrowful event compelled him to begin what would become more than one thousand hours creating a model of old Comiskey using balsa, hickory, and pine wood, aluminum, acrylic glass, plaster, other materials, and a lot of heart.

A graphic artist by trade, Wolf was, as a child of the South Shore neighborhood, in love with baseball and the making of models to embellish his train sets—little bridges, things like that.

The death of old Comiskey set loose his big-model building passions. He later made in miniature the bleachers at Wrigley Field—and then started a room-size model of the entire stadium, a task chronicled in the delightful film *Wrigley Field: Beyond the Ivy*, made locally by Bougainville Productions, which previously made a film about the wrecking of old Comiskey.

The Wrigley film took four years to make and combines real and composite characters. Watching it gives one a sharp taste of some of the frustrations of Wolf's calling: having to remove windows and brackets to get his Wrigley model out of his condo; being unable, for a time, to find a buyer.

He will soon complete his model of Fenway, which is the oldest ballpark still standing but is scheduled to be replaced by 2003. He hopes to find a buyer for this one as well.

Wolf eventually sold his Wrigley to Murphy's Bleachers, the popular bar across the street from Wrigley, where it remains on display for crowds well acquainted with baseball passions—and frustrations.

APRIL 7, 2002

CHICAGO, UNPLUGGED

At the corner of Wabash Avenue and Jackson Boulevard one recent icy afternoon, as last-minute Christmas shoppers scurried about and afternoon commuters hustled home, this slice of the city was so alive with noise—from the elevated trains above to the traffic horns below—that I couldn't help but think what it must have been like hundreds of years ago at this place on some summer day, when the only sound was the wind whipping through prairie grass.

Try that the next time an ambulance is siren-ing your way, a car's stereo is blasting, an "L" train is screeching, a jackhammer is rhythmically pounding, a couple is screaming, and a street-corner saxophone is blaring. All at once. Or maybe you won't have to seek shelter in some reverie. Perhaps you are already "safe" from the sounds of the city and are grooving to whatever is piping into your head via your iPod or one of the less-popular MP3 players.

We are not scientists, Osgood and I, nor are we pollsters, but we are sure that with each passing month, we are seeing an increasing number of people living the plugged-in public life. (Cell-phone users don't count because they often have to interrupt calls due to a passing bus or other audio intrusion).

The city is becoming divided into camps: those who are willing to take the city for what it sounds like, and those who have decided to create their own soundtrack. Of course, there are others, those who cannot hear.

Mike Leonard, the NBC *Today* show correspondent, author (*The Ride of Our Lives: Roadside Lessons of an American Family*), and astute observer of life, maintains that people do not whistle anymore, or at least as much as they used to. He's right. I have been listening.

Most of the music we unplugged people hear on the streets comes from musicians of varying ability. Until 1983, street musicians were outlawed unless they had a one-time-only permit. That law was hardly enforced (and you know that, if you ever visited the old Maxwell Street market and heard Little Walter, Robert Nighthawk, and Bo Diddley). It was eventually lifted, but subsequent ordinances, meant to be enforced by the Chicago Department of Environment and the Chicago Police Department, have made it harder for these musical entrepreneurs to find our ears.

But how pleasant it can be to encounter the flutes played by Patrick Taylor, especially in the rush-rush of commuting that takes place at O'Hare International Airport, where Osgood snapped his photo. And it is joyful to hear the way rain hits the Bean in Millennium Park, or the wind whips the flags on the Michigan Avenue Bridge.

Yes, sometimes there are, even in winter, musicians at each side of the bridge, and, yes, some people think what they are playing is noise.

Noise? It's life.

JANUARY 13, 2008

WRITERS MUSIC

A few weeks before her February 18 birthday, Zeta Moore, a sophomore at Highland Park High School, was asked by her parents what she wanted for a present. "A typewriter," she said. This was not what her parents, lawyer Keith Moore and actress Natalie West Moore, expected. Like her younger brother, Jack, Zeta is a hip kid. "It just came to me. I had never used one before," she says. "A friend has one in her house, but it doesn't work. The only time I've seen them in action is in old movies."

Not many places still sell typewriters, but among the finest in the country that do is the Independence Business Machines shop, run by Steve Kazmier, at 1623 West Montrose Avenue. That is where, a decade ago, I bought the handsome gray Olivetti portable that sits on my desk at the *Chicago Tribune,* as exotic and intriguing to visitors and some younger reporters as a shrunken head.

If you have never heard it, or it has been pushed from your brain by the soulless tapping of computer keys, the sound of typewriter keys banging is a beautiful noise. There is not a newspaper person of a certain age who does not feel this way. A typewriter's sound can evoke the charming chaos that used to exist in newsrooms. It is the sound of effort, of work.

Zeta's mother visited Kazmier's store and, after a bit of conversation about machines, bought her a handsome portable made fifty or so years ago by Antares Parva, an Italian company.

"It was awesome," Zeta says. "I just wanted to sit down and start typing, start writing."

From the time she first learned to put pen to paper, Zeta has always been a writer of great energy and creativity.

"I find that I am doing a lot more writing since I got the typewriter," she says. "And I really do think that my writing is better on the typewriter. And it looks better, too."

The love that a parent feels for a child can be measured in all sorts of ways. This is one, from Zeta's dad: "Right now I am sitting in my home office working on my computer. There is a permanently closed door that separates me from Zeta's bedroom. She has set up her typewriter on her desk, so separated by this door, I am only about four or five feet away from her. I can hear through the door that she's at her desk right now, typing. There's some techno-rock music playing in the background, along with the wonderful, familiar sound of a typewriter banging away, with the occasional but inevitable little 'ding,' followed by the 'rrrrugh.' But here's the best part: The sound is punctuated by irregular, unpredictable silences…when the typing stops, sometimes for a moment or two, sometimes for longer. It is so palpable. I can practically feel her, so close to me through the door, thinking, rereading, inspired…."

APRIL 5, 2009

A BRIEF HISTORY OF TIM

Tim Samuelson for mayor! Oh, it's too late for that, or maybe too early, or maybe just too silly. Surely Samuelson, who is currently employed—and having a great deal of fun—as the cultural historian for the City of Chicago, would dismiss such a notion. But there is not a person more in love with the city than he is, and loving the city would seem a solid qualification for running it.

I was reminded of this a few weeks ago as I listened to Samuelson charm, inform, enlighten, and entertain crowds of more than two hundred for two events at the Music Institute of Chicago's Nichols Hall in Evanston, where Osgood took the accompanying photo.

Talking about the Columbian Exposition of 1893 and the Century of Progress in 1933–34, Samuelson gave the audiences a palpable sense of Chicago's two world's fairs. Especially exciting was his tale of discovering the long-buried foundations of the giant Ferris Wheel that was the most popular attraction at the 1893 fair.

Samuelson grew up in Rogers Park, graduated from Roosevelt University with a degree in English, and was later a Loeb Fellow at the Harvard University Graduate School of Design. He went to work for the city's Commission on Chicago Historical and Architectural Landmarks, and then moved on to become curator of architecture and design at the Chicago Historical Society (now the Chicago History Museum) before taking his current job.

When he received a 2004 Studs Terkel Humanities Service Award, presented by the Illinois Humanities Council, the citation called him "an advocate for the preservation of buildings that represent diverse aspects of the city's cultural history....He possesses a wealth of knowledge about Chicago's neighborhoods; the people, the stores, the factories, the labor history. He loves to disperse this history by presenting Chicago Neighborhood Tours and by organizing exhibitions that portray subjects relating to popular culture and architecture in an accessible way."

One of the most memorable of those exhibitions was devoted to Popeil and Ronco products. That's another area of his expertise. He has been collecting such items as the Veg-O-Matic, Pocket Fisherman, Smokeless Ashtray, Buttoneer, Mr. Microphone, and many other gizmos for fifteen years. He was asked by the prestigious publishing house Rizzoli International to write a book about his collection, and the result was 2002's *But Wait! There's More!* a terrific combination of scholarship and fun.

Samuelson lives in Hyde Park with his wife, the beautiful and adventurous artist Barbara Koenen, in an apartment that offers beautiful views of the lake and is filled with all manner of things created by the great architect Louis Sullivan. Samuelson and his friend Chris Ware, the renowned graphic artist, are collaborating on a Sullivan exhibition that will eventually grace the Cultural Center, long, long before the next mayoral election.

MARCH 25, 2007

FIT FOR OFFICE

Osgood, as you can see from the dramatic photo, was among the many, many people who traveled from Chicago to Washington, D.C., to be part of the inaugural festivities. Like so, so many others, he didn't get close to the incoming president, Barack Obama. "I ended up near the Washington Monument, 1.2 miles from the Capitol, and just outside the Mall. I wasn't even able to see the Capitol except on a JumboTron," he says. "But it was thrilling, this vast ocean of people. A few yards away, someone waved a long pole with two flags, one American, the other Canadian. In another direction was a small Puerto Rican flag."

It was an amazing experience, he told me, and so I shared a story about the last time I saw Obama, which was a few weeks ago. We were only inches apart.

The president and I belong to the same South Side health club, and he was a regular visitor, mostly in the mornings. Before he won the Democratic nomination, his security detail was modest; only a couple of stern-looking guys were visible.

But after that, the building and its hallways became alive with Secret Service bodies. A pleasant woman with a metal-detecting wand checked those entering the club, and a fine-looking and friendly German shepherd, who had expertise in detecting explosives, eyed us.

As one of the other early morning exercisers observed, "This is either the safest health club in the world or the most dangerous."

Obama always wore a dark sweatshirt and pants and a hat. He did a bit of work on a treadmill, messed around with a few of the weight machines, and stretched. He rarely stayed more than about thirty minutes.

The unwritten rule of the club, before and after the election, was that Obama was not to be bothered, and most of us adhered. There would be an exchanged hello nod here and there, and sometimes one of the bolder members would say something. There were some "Congratulations" and applause in the days after the primaries and the general election.

Now things have returned to normal at the club.

"I am so glad he's in Washington," says a club member. "Not just because we can relax around here, but because I think he'll do a great job."

But never again will Obama be able to partake of the hanging-around-with-the-regular-folks intimacy he had at our club. "He always seemed kind of relaxed," says one of the regulars. "But when you think about it, it was pretty amazing to watch a president sweat."

Given the messes he has inherited and the heavy lifting he now has to do, that certainly won't be the last time.

MARCH 8, 2009

TEACHERS' PETS

In the hard heart of the city's West Side, where vacant lots stretch in all directions, sits the Michael Faraday School, named for an English chemist and physicist who died four years before the Chicago Fire of 1871. One recent frigid morning, in the parking lot next to the school on Madison Street, five cars pull in carrying seven women and three dogs.

They are all volunteers for an organization called Sit Stay Read! that for five years has been bringing the joys of reading to little kids, and using dogs as a tool.

"Reading aloud is a critical component of early childhood literacy, but reading in front of classmates can be an ordeal," says MaryEllen Schneider, the group's executive director. "We provide the children with listeners who are attentive and nonjudgmental—our dogs."

Sit Stay Read! was started in 2003 by Schneider, a former dog trainer, and Sarah Murphy, the former director of marketing for Shedd Aquarium. Its mission is fueled by sad statistics: On average, a child growing up in a middle-class family will have the benefit of as many as seventeen-hundred hours of one-on-one picture-book reading before he or she enters school, while the child in a low-income family will have twenty-five hours.

"We want to go where we will have the most impact," says Schneider. "The dogs increase confidence and generate excitement about reading."

Excitement is all over the faces of the kids in the second-grade Faraday classroom. It is a bright and colorful room. As the dogs and people enter, there are smiles on the faces of the twelve students. This is a small gathering by the standards of Sit Stay Read!, which often visit with as many as thirty-two kids.

Today's book is *The Lucky Puppy*. "It is all part of a text-to-world connection," says Schneider. "Read about a dog. See a dog. Touch a dog."

The school's principal, Shirley Scott, visits the room and says, "This has a tremendous impact."

Faraday is lucky. Some thirty people/dog teams and almost one hundred other volunteers visit eight schools in the city, but the waiting list now numbers thirty schools and is growing as word spreads. If you have a dog (Sit Stay Read! will work with each team to prepare for the classroom), or spare time, or extra money, go to www.sitstayread.org.

The results are palpable and rewarding. In the hour that the Sit Stay Read! people and dogs are in the Faraday classroom, each child gets individual attention from the people/dog teams and other, dogless, volunteers called book buddies. It is just that attention that Jaylin Hargrove (in Osgood's photo) is getting from Lisa Wiersma and her dog, Turner. One of the dogs, a cute Bichon named Wrigley, gives each kid a hug after his or her reading session. Watching this, it is impossible not to feel happy and hopeful. The kids? They just giggle and keep on reading.

MARCH 30, 2008

SIZZLE—AND YES, STEAK

At many of the area's restaurants, a ritual takes place many times during dinner and, sometimes, lunch. It involves a waiter or waitress displaying for customers a platter of raw meat, various cuts wrapped in plastic. Sometimes the platter also contains a lobster tail. Perhaps this was once helpful to those who had never seen a filet or rib eye. Perhaps it is of assistance to someone out to impress a date. We think it's just silly ceremony. At Elliott's Seafood Grille and Chop House, 6690 North Northwest Highway, in the Edison Park neighborhood, there is no such pretension, even though the owner could give a university lecture on meat.

His name is Alex Elliott. That's him in Osgood's photo, standing with his daughter Jennifer.

"I have raised them, butchered them, and cooked them," he says, forgetting to mention, though it really goes without saying, that he also now buys and sells steaks at a five-hundred-or-so-per-week clip.

On the walls of this restaurant are family photos—of weddings and other events in this Greek-Irish clan—that stretch back long before 1939, when the family opened what would be the very popular Elliott's Pine Log restaurant in Skokie.

"I did grow up in this business," Elliott says. "I can remember hanging around with my father and him spewing out all these business concepts: 'Buy the best products, never cheat your customers.' I was only twelve, but it sank in. Even now, I'm always thinking, 'What would Dad do?'"

His daughter, sitting next to him at a table, has heard this before, maybe hundreds of times. But she is smiling, and the affection and understanding between father and daughter (she has worked at other restaurants and is married to Steven Hartenstein, the chief financial officer of the Phil Stefani food empire) is palpable.

"I quit twice and was fired once," Jennifer says, with a laugh. "Or was it fired twice and quit once?" She can remember saying often as a little girl, "Daddy, I want to go to work with you," and doing so.

After the Pine Log closed in 1988, Elliott did some restaurant consulting, turned down a lot of offers to partner in restaurants, and continued to raise Black Angus cattle at the family home/farm in tiny Ringwood, near Wonder Lake, until moving closer to Chicago.

But the restaurant business is like a narcotic, and, due mainly to Jennifer's entreaties, he decided to get back into that precarious racket, opening Elliott's in 2001. "I did not do this to become a millionaire," he says. "I wanted an upscale neighborhood place where I could enjoy the customers."

That is what he has created, a charming spot at once sophisticated and laid back. The bar business is steady and lively. The dinner crowd is a nice mix of ages and occasions. Alex is there every night, Jennifer three nights a week. And the food?

"This steak is fantastic!" says Osgood.

FEBRUARY 8, 2009

PUTTING DOWN ROOTS

Chicago's motto no longer makes sense. *Urbs in horto* means "City in a garden," and for all the nice parks, medians, and golf courses around, the Chicago area is a lot more concrete than grass. But there are gardens in the city, and among the most important is City Escape. It is actually a garden and design center, meaning it's a commercial enterprise, and sits amid one of those beaten-up neighborhoods where any flash of color, not to mention a new business, is a sign of renewal and a cause for hope. It is at 3022 West Lake Street, a few blocks east of Garfield Park, part of a vast area stigmatized by the riots that followed the assassination of Rev. Martin Luther King Jr. in 1968, and subsequent decades of neglect.

One recent afternoon, a woman from the suburbs was wandering through the grounds, which are dominated by a stunning, seventeen-thousand-square-foot, Belgian-made glass-and-steel greenhouse.

She came upon Connie Rivera, who was tending to some plants.

"Can I help you?" Rivera asked.

"Yes," the woman said. "I want to meet the crazy person who built a glass house on the West Side."

"Well," Rivera said, "that would be me."

Rivera, looking over a hanging chenille plant in Osgood's photo, is a native of Michigan and was, for many years, a successful executive for nonprofit organizations until she decided to "follow my passion." She started doing her homework, interviewing landscape designers and architects, and going to work at Gethsemane Garden Center, the sprawling North Side operation.

She studied demographics, looked at maps, drove the area. Finally she found what she needed—2.4 acres at a price she could manage—and opened for business in 2003 as a seasonal operation. Now, the City Escape Garden Center & Design Studio is open year-round, seven days a week. "It's ten minutes from downtown, just off the [Eisenhower] expressway," said Rivera, who lives in the West Loop. "People have found us and return again and again."

Many who do have also explored the nearby park and its interesting marketplace. "It has been great. This business is all about inspiring people, whether for their own gardens or for this neighborhood," said Rivera, who has made it a point to hire from the area.

One of those is twenty-year-old Henry Edwards, watering plants in Osgood's photo. He had just been expelled from high school when he came calling three years ago. "We took a chance. We gave him a structured environment, a place to learn a trade," Rivera said. "Every day was not a cakewalk, but he's now a college student with a future."

JULY 22, 2007

LITERARY LIONESS

The sky burst with a vicious summer storm. People scattered for shelter in the building corridors of that portion of the South Loop known as Printers Row, some hiding under the tents that made up the area's annual June weekend book fair. One of the stars of the weekend, Karen Abbott, didn't make it out of the rain, and so, after the storm moved on, she walked into the fair's headquarters with her print silk dress soaked tight to her skin, her hair soggy and tangled.

By the time she arrived at her appointed tent, she was surprised to find more than two hundred people, a standing-room-only crowd.

"We love you here, Karen," said one water-logged man, white hair pasted to his forehead.

She loves it here. Posing for Osgood, she said, "What would I be without Chicago?"

A native of Pennsylvania, Abbott was a freelance writer living in Atlanta with her husband when she started digging into her family's history. Researching the story of a great-grandaunt, who vanished forever after arriving in Chicago from Pittsburgh in 1905, Abbott encountered a pair of savvy entrepreneurs. Minna and Ada Everleigh ran the Everleigh Club on Chicago's South Side. Though it existed for little more than a decade, starting in 1900, it was the most opulent and famous brothel in the world.

Her book about them, and the other nutty characters who populated the sinful Levee district, is titled *Sin in the Second City: Madams, Ministers, Playboys, and the Battle for America's Soul.*

Published in 2007, it exceeded the expectations of Abbott and her publisher, Random House, becoming a best seller and making Abbott a popular guest at local literary gatherings.

She now lives in New York City and comes back here often, to talk to book clubs and visit bookstores and libraries; sometimes she will drop in to see pals at the Billy Goat Tavern. Her appearance at the book fair coincided with the publication of the paperback edition of her book, which contains some tantalizing new material.

In Manhattan, she lives in an apartment not much larger than a respectable Chicago closet. She is busy: interviewing people, plowing through old newspapers, retracing footsteps made decades ago. This is all in an effort to bring to life Gypsy Rose Lee, the famous burlesque star.

"I am having a great time with this and have already started the writing," Abbott said. "But the little apartment I live in is just around the corner from the large place where Minna and Ada lived after they left Chicago and retired with their millions."

"There's just no getting away from them," she said. After a pause and a smile, she added, "But then why would I ever want to?"

August 17, 2008

RUGGED CROSS

In autumn 1963, members of the Ku Klux Klan burned a wooden cross on the lawn in front of the home of Rev. Edwin King, the white chaplain of historically African-American Tougaloo College in Jackson, Mississippi. This act of cowardly intimidation came in reaction to King's efforts in organizing a kneel-in campaign by students to desegregate Sunday morning worship services at churches in the city. It was one of many horrors suffered by King, a protégé of civil rights leader Medgar Evers' and a man who has been called "the most visible white activist in the Mississippi civil rights movement."

He was arrested and jailed and beaten many times before and after the cross burning. Six days after Evers was assassinated, in 1963, a car in which King was riding was run off the road by a car driven by the son of a rabid segregationist. His face smashed through the windshield, and as he lay bleeding, he could hear the laughter of the white members of the crowd that surrounded the wrecked car and bodies.

He was heavily bandaged when he carried the charred cross to Pittsburgh for a demonstration at a 1964 Methodist conference seeking to put an end to the church's segregated structure. There he presented it to his friend, Rev. Gerald Forshey, a local minister who was among those who had traveled from Chicago to Mississippi to help in the kneel-in efforts.

Forshey took the cross back to the La Grange home he shared with his wife, Florence. Eager to have these remains transformed into something that might endure, he enlisted the gifts of sculptor Jack Kearney, who would later be renowned for his animal sculptures made from car bumpers that dot the city. The result was the stunning and heartbreaking piece, *Crucifixion*, which you see in Osgood's photo.

Forshey died in May, and, as was his wish, the cross will now have a permanent home at the First United Methodist Church at the Chicago Temple, which crowns the building at the southeast corner of Clark Street and Washington Boulevard.

In ceremonies Sunday, the sculpture will be unveiled.

"We are honored that the cross will have a home here," says Rev. Philip Blackwell, senior pastor of the church. "It is not just a symbol but a powerful reminder."

Rev. King will attend the ceremonies. He still lives in Mississippi, still carries the scars of that long-ago crash, and spends much of his time lecturing on his experiences in the civil rights movement.

Also expected are two former Tougaloo College students who participated in the 1963 kneel-in. They now live in the Chicago area and will surely have their memories sparked on Sunday, vivid memories of a time and a place where fear and fire proved no match for faith.

SEPTEMBER 28, 2008

A HORSE WITH NO NAME

A big, brown horse stands facing east on the sidewalk in the 1700 block of West Chicago Avenue. It is a quarter horse. It is made of fiberglass. It has no name. There is another nameless fiberglass horse in the neighborhood, suspended in air, smaller but no less impressive. That horse—the one in the photograph—is a palomino. It signals to all who see it (the quarter horse being easy to miss if you are driving, because it can be hidden behind parked cars) that they have arrived at Alcala's Western Wear.

This is a remarkable place, opened in 1972 by Luis Alcala, who came here from Durango, Mexico. Alcala's was tiny then, occupying what is now the ladies department of a sprawling emporium that contains a vast assortment of things Western: shirts, leather coats, vests, belts, hats, saddles, jewelry, and bolo ties. Not to mention ten thousand pairs of boots, give or take a few dozen.

The store expanded and sales soared during the urban cowboy fad of the 1970s and early '80s. And though there may no longer be saloons in town featuring mechanical bulls, the feet of a surprising number of city folk are in boots.

"A lot of people spend all their work time in coats and ties—a work uniform," says Richard Alcala. "Jeans and boots are relaxed. Western clothes sort of signify independence."

Richard and his brother, Robert, are Luis Alcala's sons, and they now run the store. They started working there while growing up around the corner and attending Wells High School.

The store attracts people from across the country and, given the crowd that packed Alcala's one recent Saturday afternoon, a number of tourists from around the globe.

Out on the street, most people pass by Alcala's wearing what would be considered sensible shoes. Few of these people even glance in the store windows, and fewer pay attention to the quarter horse and the palomino. Most of those who shop in this neighborhood live in this neighborhood, and have become immune to the horses' novelty.

But often elderly women will stop and give the brown horse a pat, "and then whisper something to it," says Richard Alcala. "And little kids will cry if their parents don't put them up on the horse."

The horse has been standing on the sidewalk for fifteen years. People have tried to buy it—and they have, sort of. Alcala's has supplied about a half-dozen copies, at "about fifteen hundred dollars, including shipping."

Richard Alcala isn't sure what the buyers have done with these horses. He assumes they are "sitting on lawns someplace"—their eyes frozen forever, perhaps, on some suburban horizon.

SEPTEMBER 20, 1998

OF QUIET LIVES

It is jarring to see Robert Wolf in the urban setting in which he was captured on film by Osgood, because Wolf, who did a lot of writing for the *Chicago Tribune* some time back, has been living a rural life for years. Wolf lives in the northeastern corner of Iowa with his wife, Bonnie Koloc, the legendary folk singer. For the last decade, Wolf has been getting people to tell him stories, and the harvest is the rich and satisfying *An American Mosaic: Prose and Poetry by Everyday Folk* (Oxford University Press).

Those "everyday folk" are the homeless and day laborers, farmers and teachers, college students and commercial fishermen. They met Wolf during the many writing workshops he conducts. He gets people to attend by telling them "anyone who can tell a story can write one." That's a bold theory. But the book is filled with wonderful stories. Almost all are interesting, and some of them are poetic. Here's a bit from a story by a farmer named Richard Sandry:

> We finally get home and just as we come into the house, the rain begins to fall. Shortly the full fury of the storm is upon us. As I watch, looking out through the window, I think of how the days of my life go. How the clouds on the horizon of my sunrises sometimes, later in the day, turn into the black clouds of fear, of despair, of anger, of uncertainty, and of depression.

The stories in this book, and in one called *River Days*, both of which also contain lovely artwork by Koloc, and essays and commentary by Wolf, are funny, sad, and meaningful. They offer insights into the lives of people and places that many of us, caught up in the frenetic pace of city life, forget exist.

They are stories of small towns and quiet lives.

SEPTEMBER 12, 1999

TURKEY IN THE RAW

To hear an owner of one of the city's dozen or so live-poultry stores tell it, more and more people are interested in fresh birds, even if they aren't interested in seeing them prepared. Call me squeamish, but walking into Chicago Live Poultry, 3057 West Lawrence Avenue, and seeing all sorts of animals—rabbits, pigeons, turkeys, geese, roosters, quail, guinea hens, and chickens, lots of chickens—sitting in cages and unknowingly awaiting their inevitable place on someone's dinner table was almost enough to instantly convert me to vegetarianism.

Osgood and I entered this store because we had been attracted by its windows, which are covered with colorful paintings of animals, the sort of playful illustrations one might find in a children's book.

The store has been around more than fifteen years, according to Hibib Alshimary, who started working there as a young man and who is now one of the owners. It is one of only about a dozen live-poultry retail shops in the Chicago area.

This, of course, is the shop's busiest season. During this month, Chicago Live Poultry prepares and sells some fifty turkeys a week.

The process by which this is accomplished is not for the fainthearted. But let's not be hypocritical: It is the same process employed, in a more mechanized and automated fashion, by such huge poultry companies as Tyson and Perdue. Which is the more gruesome?

Osgood took many pictures of birds being beheaded, plucked, and cleaned. He is not at all squeamish. But many people buying birds and rabbits did not want to have their names appear in the paper, lest they, as one customer puts it, "have people think that we are cruel or weird or something."

"Does it bother me to kill the animals? No way," Alshimary says. "This is a good, fast-growing business."

In fact, business is so good (the store sells, Alshimary says, something in the neighborhood of 450 chickens a week) that he has opened another store in the area of Devon and Western Avenues.

"The people like the food because it is fresher," he says. "The animals are raised without any chemicals. People who buy here tell their friends, and they tell others. Many yuppies come now."

Wherever I am at Thanksgiving, there will probably be a turkey, too. And, memories of being in a poultry store nicely faded, I'll probably have some. I just hope it's one I haven't met.

NOVEMBER 22, 1998

LEON IN WINTER

They gather yearly—no matter the weather, the creaks in their bones, or the increasing fog of some of their memories—at 10:00 AM on March 13 at a bridge in Jackson Park to honor Clarence Darrow, the most famous lawyer of the century just passed. A marvelously diverse group of students, lawyers, politicians, curiosity seekers, civil libertarians, and history buffs (as seen in Osgood's photo), they do this at the Clarence Darrow Bridge, just to the south of the Museum of Science and Industry. The date marks the anniversary of Darrow's death in 1938 (he was born on April 18, 1857, 150 years ago last Wednesday). The bridge, which was visible from Darrow's home, where he died at age eighty, was a place the attorney frequently went alone to think, to contemplate the mysteries of life and the complexities of his cases, such as the still-famous Chicago murder trial of Nathan Leopold and Richard Loeb, who killed fourteen-year-old Bobby Franks, and his defense of John T. Scopes' right to teach the theory of evolution in a Tennessee public school.

Following services at Bond Chapel on the University of Chicago campus, Darrow's ashes were scattered over the lagoon from the bridge, but it was not until 1957, when the city's relatively new mayor, Richard J. Daley, dedicated the bridge in Darrow's name, that people started the March 13 gatherings.

There are some who believe that the spirit of Darrow prowls this area. Darrow, famously agnostic, had said before his death that, if in fact there was an afterlife, he would return to the bridge on the date of his death. He did this, in part, to help debunk the mediums, popular at the time, who made money pretending to summon the dead.

Darrow made clear his feelings on an afterlife: "Every man knows when his life began....If I did not exist in the past, why should I, or could I, exist in the future?"

This year, as in years past, a wreath was tossed upon the waters of the lagoon and, after a few words, the crowd went into the museum for a formal discussion of Darrow's legacy.

This is one of the city's quiet events, rarely covered anymore by the news media.

Who needs ghosts when you've got Leon Despres, who came to the Darrow bridge more times than even her could remember? That's him in the wheelchair in Osgood's shot.

"Nobody thinks that anybody will live to be one hundred..." he said a few years later, pausing. "Including me."

It was a few weeks before the arrival of that milestone, which comes on February 2 and is scheduled to be accompanied by all manner of festivities, including a breakfast gathering of some of his buddies at the University Club, where he swam every morning for decades until having to give that up four years ago, and a guitar concert in his apartment. Despres deserves the attention. A lawyer, teacher, fighter for good causes, his most public battles came between 1955 and 1975. As the Fifth Ward's alderman in the City Council, he was one of very few opposition voices against Mayor Richard J. Daley and his potent machine. He has long been called "the conscience of the city."

In his large apartment, he looked out the window: a beautiful view across snow-covered Jackson Park toward the lake. He has lived here for twenty years, a place filled with warmth and things of meaning. But some were missing—more than a dozen paintings recently donated to the Smart Gallery, among them a portrait of his wife, Marian, by Diego Rivera. "The crown jewel of our collection," Despres said.

And she is the greatest absence: Marian Despres—civic activist, preservationist—died last January. They had been married since 1931 and met Rivera in 1938. This story also involves the delivery of a suitcase—and such has been the novelistic nature of Despres' life—to Leon Trotsky, the exiled Bolshevik who was then living in Mexico.

There are still Rivera drawings in the apartment, Marian is still in her husband's heart. And he stays busy. He has twenty-four-hour-a-day care, a desk piled with correspondence, and a table filled with books. "I read. I write. I pay close attention to politics," he said, recalling his relationship with Barack Obama's political adviser, David Axelrod.

"I did a radio program with David on the University of Chicago station," he said. "David was a good student, though I think I indulged him. The show? To this day I have never found anyone who ever heard it."

So many people, so many stories.

It is impossible, in these pages, to detail this life and so it is good to have a new book, *Chicago Afternoons with Leon: 99½ Years Old and Looking Forward*, written with former *Chicago Tribune* reporter Kenan Heise.

"The thing is to stay engaged in life," Despres said, looking out the window at the shadows of bare trees easing their way along the snow.

THE COP SHOP

Some of my police-officer friends I don't see often enough. I will occasionally run into Mike at a nearby tavern where he unwinds after his shift. He used to be a newspaper photographer but gave that up for—no offense meant to Osgood or the other fine photographers here—a higher calling. And Bill married a lovely girl named Jenny and moved far south, so I only see him when I'm invited over for a barbecue.

Understandably, I have been thinking about these guys a lot since September, and that, perhaps, is why I decided to do some of my Christmas shopping at the headquarters of the police officers union, the Fraternal Order of Police, Chicago Lodge Number 7, 1412 West Washington Boulevard. On the first floor of the building is, perhaps, the city's most unusual gift shop.

The FOP opened its store in 1996, and in the weeks before Christmas, business was brisk.

"But we still don't get many members of the public," said the woman behind the counter, as she counted up my purchases, which included a teddy bear dressed as a cop.

There are a lot of gift options, as well as practical items for the working cop. There are cool jackets, mugs, glasses, military figures, T-shirts, toys, hats (some with NYPD logos), scarves, jewelry, books, and many things Irish-themed. Most items are straightforward, but some of the T-shirts have naughty messages, such as "You...Me, Whipped Cream, Handcuffs, Any Questions?"

One thing that might startle a civilian shopper is the number of items adorned with pigs. "Pig," especially during the raucous 1960s, was a common insult yelled at the police. At the FOP shop, you can find pigs on T-shirts and ties.

There's also Al Capone, on a shot glass and a refrigerator magnet, with one of his famous quotes, "There are no gangsters in Chicago."

Of course there were, and there still are, and it has been the job of the police to keep them at bay or put them in jail. Sure, there are bad cops—there are bad people in any profession—but the vast majority try their best to do their jobs.

As the woman behind the counter said, "I think people this year have gotten a lot of new respect for what we do." No doubt.

JANUARY 6, 2002

EXPERIENCE THIS!

A menu touting "no beef" and "no pork" will not grab the crowd at Gibsons, but then the crowd at Gibsons isn't likely to abandon the flashy pleasures of that restaurant's Rush Street location for the Austin neighborhood, which is where it would find Quench, the Experience, at 5815 West Madison Street. One recent Saturday afternoon at the small and handsome place, a number of people were behind the counter, taking orders and working the kitchen. A steady stream of customers, of all ages, walked through the door.

In this neighborhood, fast-food outlets and mom-and-pop rib joints dominate the culinary scene. Add to that the lack of full-line grocery stores, and you know why, in these food deserts, residents suffer health problems that might be helped or even cured by a better diet.

"Some people take some convincing to try something new, but when they do, they like it," said the one waitress, who was serving eight tables and pleasantly persuaded me to try the special Quench punch with the blackened chicken sub I had ordered. Both were terrific, as was the bill, which was less than ten dollars.

The menu is filled with salads, fish, pastas, turkey concoctions, chicken, and some Mexican dishes. The breakfast menu is particularly enticing, though so far it is only served from 8:00 AM to noon on weekends. Otherwise the place is open from 11:00 AM to 10:00 PM every day but Monday, when it is closed. The most expensive thing on the menu is eleven dollars. There is artwork on the walls, some of it very colorful stuff, and a couple of iconic portraits (Barack Obama and Tiger Woods). For music, there is vintage soul and R&B, and rising over it spirited conversation.

This restaurant opened in August, joining the two others of similar name, Quench, at 510 East Seventy-fifth Street and Quench, the Evolution, at 4653 South Michigan Avenue. They, in turn, are part of the larger restaurant operation called the I Love Food Group, run by Quentin Love, who might be on his way to becoming the African-American Richard Melman, founder of the Lettuce Entertain You empire.

Love's partner in Quench, the Experience, is Shawn Taylor, fine proof that there is life after newspapers. She left the *Chicago Tribune* late in 2005 and, in an attempt to satisfy her lifelong interest in food and cooking, toyed with the idea of opening her own place or becoming a chef while starting a media-consulting firm.

She met Love, a deal was struck, the storefront location was found, and Taylor, there in Osgood's photo, now says, "The community has been so welcoming. We have a vision for this place, and it's being realized."

So look for Quench the next time you're on the West Side. It's a small place, nice sign, and right next to the venerable Mario's Butcher Shop.

NOVEMBER 30, 2008

LET IT SNOW

Winter. It snows in Chicago. It gets cold in Chicago. These facts may not come as news to most of you, but with every winter's first few slaps, a surprising number of otherwise sensible people act as if they had just been dumped here after never having set foot outside Phoenix. "Brutal out there," said one such person, walking into a Starbucks store after "suffering" the thirty-seven-degree temperature outside. Brutal? Think about it: When the temperature hits thirty-seven some March afternoon, people will think spring is just around the corner and dream of baseball's bleachers.

Winter. It snows in Chicago. It gets cold in Chicago. And people forget how to drive. They whine. Weathercasters become frenetic stars as television news programs are transformed. There are times in winter when weather deserves extensive coverage. But too often we get hyperbole and hysteria that make many yearn for the calming ways of Chicago's first famous weathercaster, P. J. Hoff. A former newspaper reporter and cartoonist who worked at WBBM-Channel 2 from 1954 to 1968, he used cartoon sketches of such characters as the "Vice President in Charge of Looking Out the Window" and "Mr. Yell 'n' Cuss."

I have only vague memories of the man because I was a kid in those days, and kids, still, thank God, don't seem to mind winter. Let it snow and they'll sled on it, make forts out of it, and pack it into small projectiles to hurl at other kids and passing buses. They'll now watch television news only to see if their school's closing is being announced in the scroll at the bottom of the screen.

But we grow up, and winter becomes something to curse. We brush the snow off our coats and heads. We shovel it, slosh through it. We suffer it. We almost never stop to appreciate the beauty of it.

The biggest wallop came with the blizzard in January 1967, the greatest single snowstorm in Chicago history. The great M. W. Newman wrote about it for the bygone *Daily News*. I reread the story every winter, and this is some of what he wrote:

> It came over the plains like a swollen fist, scooped up all of Chicago and casually tangled it in knots. The stricken metropolis lay gasping, barely able to move. The storm swatted it, slugged it, smashed it, crushed it in seventy-five-million tons of snow. But in the end the metropolis did not break. Like a dazed giant, it shuddered under the monstrous weight and began stumbling to its knees...then regained its feet.

A few paragraphs later, Newman wrote, "Tens of thousands of Chicagoans fought the storm, from the first. They met the superstorm and the storm could not break the city."

So, remember: It snows in Chicago. It gets cold in Chicago.

And we do not break.

JANUARY 20, 2008

THE OLD MAN AND THE TEE

There are trees that have been around Beverly Country Club longer than Dick Carparelli, but not many. The South Side oasis is one hundred years old this year, and for sixty-two of those years, Carparelli has been wandering its fairways, teaching the infinite particulars of golf. "He is a living institution who helps bridge all the generations at the club," says BCC member and businessman Bill Kingore. "He is also a great inspiration to me as a gentleman and friend." Kingore is the unofficial Carparelli biographer, and will happily tell you that the veteran pro was born ninety-one years ago in Harrison, New York, one of ten kids; got hooked on the game as a caddie; came to Chicago and to Beverly to work for his uncle, BCC head golf pro Charley Penna, in 1946, after flying planes for the Army Air Corps during World War II.

Carparelli has been married for sixty years to Christine. They raised a daughter, Felicia, and along with his two grandchildren, Peter and Tina, Carparelli has what he calls "as fine a family as any man could have."

He will tell you, almost in passing, that he grew up near golf great Gene Sarazen, that he saw Babe Ruth on the course ("He could play"), that the real advances in the game are not in the high-tech clubs but in ball composition, and that the most important elements of a swing are the grip and setup. "The game's not as complicated as most people like to think," he says.

It is impossible to calculate the number of golfers whose swings, and thus lives (and perhaps marriages), have been aided by Carparelli's tutelage.

He still plays "a few holes here and there, sometimes more. I don't hit it as far, but I can hit it."

He still gives a number of lessons every week. One of his most recent students was Bill Murray, who stopped in for a round of golf with some members, including business consultant Steve Coates, the day before Murray jumped out of a plane during the Chicago Air & Water Show.

"Dick is like the Joe Paterno of Beverly," Coates says. "He's there every season to coach us and cheer us on with incredibly great energy and frame of mind."

Murray needed his help. "He told me he wanted to start drawing the ball," making its path go from right to left, Carparelli says. "He's a good player. A few minutes was all it took."

Walking around the club with Carparelli, now carrying the lofty title of pro emeritus, you sense what it must be like to walk around Vatican City with the pope. Affection and reverence float through the air.

For fifty-five years, he has instructed club member Bob Moysey, eighty-six. That's the two of them, Moysey with the club, in Osgood's photo. They long ago transcended the student-teacher relationship and are close friends.

"You must have won the club championship a lot," a visitor says.

"Actually," Moysey replies, with the slyest and sweetest smile directed at Carparelli, "not yet."

SEPTEMBER 21, 2008

A LITERARY HEARTH

The smiling woman in Osgood's photo is Florence Shay, and she is sitting in the lovely literary world that is her store, Titles, Inc., 1821 St. Johns Avenue, Highland Park. I have long had a thing for old and rare books, and love the stores that sell them, and the people who own those stores. Shay, and another favorite, John LaPine of Printers Row Fine & Rare Books, 715 South Dearborn Street, both seem to understand that, as I once wrote, "the pages of an old book are warm, literally warm, as if they had captured and retained the heat of the hands that previously turned them." Or, as Shay puts it: "There is an enchantment to old books, especially ones signed by authors. It means that the writer held it in his or her hands. If that doesn't resonate with you, you are not a book lover."

The store is always a delight for book lovers, whether they are serious collectors, willing to pay the many thousands of dollars that rare and/or autographed first editions demand, or merely people browsing and touching, and, on the best days, finding an affordable gem.

The greatest thing about wandering Titles or Printers Row or any of the similar bookstores that remain, is that they allow you to be surprised, to find something you didn't even know you were looking for.

Titles has a number of books by Florence's husband, photographer-author Art Shay, one of the most ebullient people we have ever met.

Some of his books are on the shelves. He has written so many that I stopped counting at around seventy-five. Some of the best are about his great pal Nelson Algren, and some of *his* books are on the shelves, too.

Just seeing one of those books brought back the memory of the afternoon Shay almost got us both killed. He was eager to show me where Algren and Simone de Beauvoir had, in Shay's inimitable words, "shared Algren's squeaky bed." The problem was that the building in which this bed-sharing took place (1523 West Wabansia Avenue) was long gone. It had been replaced by the Kennedy Expressway. As some friendly, if incredulous, cops observed, Shay boldly tried to halt traffic so we could stand where the building and its bed once stood.

Cars honked. Cars swerved. We survived.

Titles, Inc. does not just survive; it thrives, more than thirty years after opening. Art and Florence's marriage is decades longer. Both of them, never ones to gather dust or even relax, have active blogs. On hers (indianhillmediaworks.typepad.com/titles/), you would have recently found this charming comment: "It warms the cockles of my heart (don't tell me you never heard that one) when my grandkid's hero is an author rather than a rock star."

OCTOBER 12, 2008

SOLE MAN

Altman's Men's Shoes and Boots has all manner of famous clients from the worlds of politics, show business, big business, and sports. But owner Marty Altman will not tell you who they are. "These aren't customers. They aren't clients," he says. "They are friends, and I don't throw around my friends' names."

That is one aspect of the old-school philosophy of the store, where Altman has forty-five thousand, more or less, pairs of shoes available for your walking pleasure. You will see only a few hundred of them on the shelves in Altman's cozy little shop at 120 West Monroe Street. The rest are buried, so to speak, in twenty-two (or was that twenty-three?) storage spaces below street level.

In this era of fast shopping, discount deals, and know-nothing salespeople, Altman's thrives as a reminder of personalized service and whatever-you-need-we've-got inventory. (That's Antonio Woods helping customer John Biloz, in Osgood's photo.) "Five AAAA to 20 EEEE, those are the sizes we carry," Altman says. "And maybe fifty different brands. There are very few places with that sort of inventory. But that's how we compete with the big guys."

He has been at this location for more than three decades and in the shoe business almost his entire life. His father, Jack, opened a full-service store—for men, women, and kids—at Madison Street and Cicero Avenue in 1932. He grew up in the Austin neighborhood and started working in earnest at fourteen, after his father died. He was in the shoe business with a brother and brother-in-law (the West Side store closed in 1967) before going it alone in the Loop. He is at the store every day, often with his daughter, Jackie Delott, who does bookkeeping and marketing.

"Of course it's still fun, or I wouldn't be here," says Altman, who turns seventy-two in November. "It keeps the mind sharp and the blood flowing."

"People take shoes for granted. A man will spend a thousand dollars on a suit, and then come in and think that a hundred dollars is expensive for shoes." The shoes at Altman's run from about $85 to $798, that high price for a pair of alligator "kicks."

Altman himself has only about a dozen pairs and takes great care of each, wearing a pair for no more than two days at a stretch and using shoe trees when they are in the closet.

It is possible at a place like Altman's—though there are, sadly, few places like Altman's left—to feel almost is if you're in a hands-on art gallery, examining pieces of leather (and snakeskin, alligator, lizard) sculpture. Osgood and I looked down at our own shoes, bought God knows where with only a moment's thought, and determined to each purchase a good pair soon.

SEPTEMBER 4, 2005

CHILLING OUT

You might never see a face more delighted than Osgood's was as he gleefully abandoned his straw and slurped down the last of his milkshake at the Plush Horse. "There is," he said, between slurps, "nothing like a good ice cream parlor." He is right, of course. And there may be none better than the Plush Horse, an outpost of ice cream and serenity in Palos Park. There are other such long-lived oases—Rainbow Cone on the South Side, Margie's Candies in Bucktown, Homer's in Wilmette, among them—so it is not difficult to find such a place. It is not like searching for drive-in movie theaters. And the rewards are beyond those of the palate.

It is impossible to be morose hunched over a shake, cone, or more exotic concoction.

Of all the local ice cream spots, the Plush Horse may have the deepest roots, since the building that is its home first rose on the still-bucolic corner of Eighty-sixth Avenue and 123rd Street as a

farmhouse in 1893. In time, the ground level was transformed into a general store, and later a butcher shop and the suburb's post office.

When the Itzel family bought the property in 1937, they turned the space into an ice cream parlor and called it the Hobby Horse. There have been a number of owners since, but they wisely have not tampered with its wrought-iron tables and chairs, colorful wallpaper, wood floors, high tin ceiling, or calming courtyard.

"Every Sunday we would walk across the street after going to church," says Zay Smith, a *Chicago Sun-Times* columnist who grew up in Palos Park. "We never called it the Hobby Horse or Plush Horse. A lot of people called it Itzel's but to me it was always Sophie's."

Sophie was Sophie Itzel, who worked behind the counter for decades and who, Smith recalls, "would fry you up a burger on the side."

"After church, I always had butter cream, which was butter pecan without the pecans," Smith says. "My dad had Hawaiian Delight, which was pineapples and coconut, and my mother had the hot fudge sundae."

There is great affection in his voice, and more memories flow. It all seems part of some quiet but important message: It is summer. You are not getting any younger. Go find yourself some ice cream, and a nice place to eat it.

JULY 20, 2008

MEMORY LAPSE

On the night of March 4, the birthday of the city, Timuel Black and I walked into the Congress Room on the second floor of Roosevelt University expecting to see the place packed with college kids. We were playing a small part in the nearly five-month-long series of free public programs celebrating Harold Washington that began on November 25, the twentieth anniversary of Washington's death, and ended on April 12, the twenty-fifth anniversary of his election as mayor of Chicago.

The evening was to consist of a conversation between Black, who might have known Washington as well as anyone, and me, who didn't know him well at all. Roosevelt University is where Washington and Black attended college, first met one another, and started sharing dreams of social equality and justice. The school's motto is "Dedicated to the enlightenment of the human spirit."

Black and I stared as we walked into an almost-empty room. "Do you think any more people will be coming?" he asked.

"Of course," I told him.

The Harold Washington Commemorative Year, the Illinois nonprofit corporation that created the programming series, had done a fine job of promoting its events. Ten more minutes passed. Fewer than a dozen more people came, among them Osgood, with camera. The crowd, so to speak, included photographer Marc PoKempner and journalist Salim Muwakkil, the team that helped create the magnificent book *Harold!: Photographs from the Harold Washington Years*, which was edited by Ron Dorfman and includes photos by Antonio Dickey.

So, we talked. I asked questions and Black provided answers, which engagingly took the form of long stories, crammed with humor, insight, and detail, and not a whiff of self-importance. He talked of the weekly poker games with Washington and others so evocatively that I would have eagerly sat in (even if it meant losing every hand), and of early voter-registration efforts, and of the current presidential campaign. He did not talk about his years as a social worker, high school and college teacher, union organizer, and community political activist. He did not even mention his *Bridges of Memory* books, compelling oral histories of the African-American experience in Chicago.

"I have lived a lot of the city's history," said Black, a few steps away from his ninetieth birthday but frequently out and about in public forums.

History is, of course, available by many means. There are books, documentaries, Wikipedia. But history delivered firsthand is a rare commodity, and it packs a punch that dazzles.

Sad that so few were interested in hearing about Washington from Black, a living link. We talked and then we left, walking through a lounging area littered with students who missed the "show."

One was working the buttons of his cell phone. Five were asleep.

MAY 18, 2008

INSPIRING AWE

To what surely would have been the astonishment of friends, I found myself one recent Saturday standing at the altar of Second Presbyterian Church, 1936 South Michigan Avenue. I am not a churchgoing person, but I was less intimidated than I might have been because my altar appearance had been preceded by a spirited rendition of Muddy Waters' "Got My Mojo Working," which is not what one would call a religious standard.

I was playing a small part in an event for the Tribute Markers of Distinction program, which is partly sponsored by the *Chicago Tribune*. The seven-foot-tall enamel markers contain photos and biographical information about notable Chicagoans. They started sprouting around the city in 1997 and now number sixty. They honor many famous and familiar Chicagoans, but also some of our history's hidden heroes. This year's honorees included Col. Robert R. McCormick, Marshall Field, Ben Hecht, Muddy Waters, African-American aviation pioneer Bessie Coleman, pioneer gospel music composer Thomas A. Dorsey, and Abe Saperstein, the founder of the Harlem Globetrotters.

Most of the people filling the pews had never been in the church before. They listened to some speeches, and to music from bluesman John Primer and from the Lena McLin Singers, led by Dorsey's niece.

But mostly, they marveled at the church, one of the city's oldest—built in 1874 and partly rebuilt after a 1900 fire—and most beautiful, with striking murals, sculptures, glorious Tiffany windows, dark oak wood, and a magnificent organ.

Those who do not regularly attend religious services often feel the call this time of year—to pray and thank and rejoice. Being in a place as aesthetically awe-inspiring as Second Presbyterian reminds you what an amazing creation we are, and what amazing things we are capable of creating.

DECEMBER 19, 1999

TAVERN TALES

Booze is a beautiful, dangerously seductive word. Say it. Let it burst softly from your lips: "Booze." It is a word with deep roots in this city, and deeper still in Europe, because it derives from the Middle English word *bousen*. Chicago has always been a city of big thirsts, and even as the number of taverns (a word meant, by definition of liquor licenses, to signify everything from the corner tap to the fanciest nightclub) diminished from nearly seven thousand in the early 1960s to around the one thousand mark today, we still enjoy a drink (or two or three or...) here.

There is good reason some people are referred to as "serious drinkers" and I think it has less to do with excess boozing than understanding that drinking is not a game.

Read this, my current favorite drinking-related paragraph, courtesy of Raymond Chandler in *The Long Goodbye*, which was a One Book, One Chicago selection:

> I like bars just after they open for the evening. When the air inside is still cool and clean and everything is shiny and the barkeep is giving himself that last look in the mirror to see if his tie is straight and his hair is smooth. I like the neat bottles on the bar back and the lovely shining glasses and the anticipation. I like to watch the man mix the first one of the evening and put it down on a crisp mat and put the little folded napkin beside it. I like to taste it slowly. The first quiet drink of the evening in a quiet bar— that's wonderful.

That's written by a man who knew and loved bars (and, indeed, suffered for that). Though he spent most of his early years in England, Chandler was born in Chicago in 1888. He would have fit in nicely with the then hard-drinking writing crowd had he stayed here. He understood taverns, their place in our society, our city.

So does John Wonsil, the man in the cowboy hat, who is a regular at Charlotte's Bar & Grill at 6000 West Gunnison Street on the Far Northwest Side.

Wonsil was, until recently, an employee of the *Chicago Tribune*, retiring after forty-three years in the advertising department. He is the sort of person every neighborhood tavern needs: quiet, companionable, rarely over-served, and thus no trouble at all. He is also the kind of person who needs a neighborhood tavern. "It's no fun sitting home alone," says Wonsil, who lives a few blocks from Charlotte's. "I go to the bar to play some pool, watch the Cubs or Bears. I've gotten to know a lot of the other regulars and I've come to think of them as good friends."

It used to be easy to find a neighborhood tavern. They still exist, of course, but are an endangered urban species. This has to do with changing drinking habits but is also the result of a determined effort on the part of the mayor and many aldermen to cut the number of taverns through tough new liquor licensing procedures.

Charlotte's is owned and operated by Charlotte Dolan. It is a simple and large place, with a pool table, a bunch of TV sets, some video games, a jukebox, and good bar food, along the lines of burgers and pizza.

"You get a really mixed crowd," said Wonsil. "I've made friends with motorcycle guys, construction workers. This is a peaceful and clean place. The people who come here enjoy sports, they enjoy life. It's a community and I'm glad I can be a part of it."

These communities exist all over town, even at a place as seemingly rarefied as the Pump Room, one of the city's most venerable "taverns," having opened in 1938 in the Ambassador East Hotel in the heart of the Gold Coast.

It too has its regulars and among them is Max Weismann. For nearly a decade he lived upstairs in the Ambassador East Hotel. Now he lives across the street and can be found at the Pump Room bar at least three nights a week. He is a most companionable sort, full of witty and intelligent conversation and observations. He has had an interesting life, which finds him now spending his days reading, writing, and teaching. He is the head of the Center for the Study of the Great Ideas, which he founded with his mentor, Mortimer Adler.

In style, the Gold Coast and East Side share little, but walk into O'Hara's, 3541 East 106th Street, and you will find Patti and Jim O'Hara, sister and brother, sharing stories, as Jim's wife, Darlene, is serving drinks to the regulars.

"People don't even know this is part of Chicago," says Jim, a retired Chicago Police Department lieutenant. "It's kind of like an island."

"The East Side was a great place to grow up," says Patti, seated with Jim in Osgood's photo.

East Side is the name of the neighborhood, and indeed it's pretty obscure, nestled against the state of Indiana. Jim and Patti were raised above what is now a Mexican restaurant in the building next door, but was the original O'Hara's.

The place began when their father, Joe, decided he had had enough of working in the nearby mills and in 1947 opened a package liquor store. It moved into its current spot in 1953 and Jim and Patti have wonderful memories of life above the tavern.

"Remember when we would come down and play in the bar after everybody left?" asks Patti.

"And find all that money on the floor," says Jim.

Jim also found a bride. "I was a hot property in those days," he says, smiling.

My favorite tavern, it goes without saying, is the subterranean place of red-and-white-checked tables known as the Billy Goat. It was made into a tourist attraction more than twenty years ago by those local-lads-made-good, John Belushi and Bill Murray and their *Saturday Night Live* skit modeled after the Billy Goat.

Murray has, of course, been to the Billy Goat many times before. He knows, from TV and real life, the "Cheezbooger, cheezbooger/no Pepsi, Coke/no fries, chips" routine.

So it is surprising when he walks in one day and says to waiter Tito Chacon, "How about a double cheeseburger? And a Pepsi."

"No Pepsi," says Chacon, "Coke."

"Make it a large Pepsi, then," says Murray.

His delivery is so deadpan that it is disarming. His timing is that of a person who is just naturally funny but whom also carries a slightly subversive streak. It is easy, effortless, but also edgy.

"What do you want on it?" asks Chacon.

"Just mustard and pickles," says Murray. "Tito, where are you from?"

"Mexico," says Chacon.

"Never heard of it," says Murray.

"Huh?" says Chacon.

In a matter of minutes, Chacon delivers his first double cheeseburger.

He looks down at the burger.

"What is this?" he asks, pointing.

"That's ketchup," says Chacon.

"What did you do on the test," asks Murray, "when they asked, 'What president didn't like ketchup?'"

"Huh?" asks Chacon, who suddenly realizes the mistake. "Oh, I'm sorry. I get you a new one. You didn't want the ketchup."

"I'll have to have you fired," says Murray.

Through the door walks Sam Sianis, the owner of Billy Goat, who immediately recognizes Murray and heads to his table.

"Sam," says Murray, getting out of his chair. "I saw that new place of yours over by the United Center. For a minute I thought they'd run you out of here."

"No, no," says Sianis. "I got four places now."

"You're the most successful Greek in the world," Murray says.

HANG 'EM HIGH

A photographer came into the *Chicago Tribune* offices more than four years ago. His name was Loren Santow, and he had taken pictures of shoes hanging from various tall objects, such as telephone wires and poles and trees. I wrote a story to accompany the photos, and I have not since been able to travel about without constantly scanning the skies.

I've seen plenty of hanging shoes in the city, and, indeed, the phenomenon seems primarily urban. So I was recently stunned to see a Highland Park tree loaded with shoes. Built on what was the site of two Potawatomi villages, Highland Park is among the area's most beautiful suburbs, with a lakeshore, bluffs, woods, and ravines.

It is also home to Ravinia park, and I recall the time I took my shoes off and went walking across the grass during a long-ago Janis Joplin concert. Now I wonder if I ever retrieved those shoes before going home. (I was young and foolish in those days.)

Could these shoes of more recent vintage have been stolen from the Ravinia lawn last summer by some youthful pranksters?

How long has this shoe tree been here?

What does it mean?

Osgood and I asked the few people passing by—it was still cold when we were there—and none had an answer to those questions.

This frustrated Osgood, who wants answers to all questions. But it was okay with me. There is not, I figure, enough mystery in this world, and even one as small and insignificant as this one makes life a little more interesting.

When I wrote about Santow's photographs of hanging shoes four years ago, many readers responded with theories. Some said the shoes were meant to mark gang territory. Some said they signified places to buy drugs.

Surely some Highland Park resident knows the story behind the shoe tree. Maybe he or she will call or write and let me know: "The shoes are there because..."

And that information will, in some small way, ruin my day.

MAY 6, 2001

GAITED COMMUNITY

Dana Montana, one of the most fascinating and nicest people we have ever met, has embarked on a new adventure that colorfully blends her expertise in the entertainment business with her lifelong passion for horses. It is, actually, two adventures in one: the Dancing Horses Dinner Theater and Animal Gardens, both of which share forty lovely Wisconsin acres between Lake Geneva and Delavan.

"I fell in love with horses when I was a little girl and came to Wisconsin to visit my grandparents," she says. "This has always been my dream, to have a place where I could share my love and let people see these magnificent horses. We allow the horses to do all sorts of amazing things."

The show is eye-poppingly pleasing, but then Montana has always known how to put on a show. At first, she was it, in a sense, as one of the first gang of Playboy Bunnies, working at the original Playboy Club on Walton Street in the early 1960s. Divorced and with three young children to support, she later bought a roadside tavern near Lake Geneva that she named the Sugar Shack. For a time, the place featured what were then known as strippers. One of her performers was Sally Rand, the legendary diversion of the 1933 Chicago World's Fair, who was still fan dancing well into her sixties.

Then one night nearly thirty years ago, Montana decided that what the world needed was nude male dancers. As she told me long ago: "It wasn't that I was into women's lib or anything like that. I just thought I knew women wanted a little sex in their lives. The problem is that the word 'sex' has these bad definitions for people."

The place, the idea, was a sensation, leading to articles in national magazines, national TV appearances, and busloads of giggling women intent on innocent fun.

Montana raised those three kids, two daughters and a son, but she was never lucky in love. "I am through with men forever," she told me more than a decade ago, and she has been true to that vow.

Where would she find the time? She works seven days a week.

The Sugar Shack, which now features male and female dancers, though never in the same room at the same time, will soon host its one-millionth patron.

Most of them have been women from the Chicago area, and now many of them are bringing their husbands and kids to the Dancing Horses Dinner Theater to witness an extravagant indoor production with music, lights, and plenty of action: Think Las Vegas, or Cirque du Soleil.

It runs on weekends through the end of the year. The Animal Gardens, which feature a bird show, walking trail, petting zoo, and other wild kingdom treats, will be open only until the end of the month, when the cold weather starts inching into Wisconsin.

OCTOBER 21, 2007

GETTING A GRIP

There are hundreds, likely thousands, of personal trainers in the Chicago area, and Barbara Queen is almost certainly the only one to ever play Carnegie Hall. She did so more than twenty years ago, when she was a young classical violinist in Manhattan. Though she also played in orchestras on Broadway and on tours to Japan, she had a lot of other jobs to make ends meet. Mostly she waitressed, then took a job at a health club.

"I found myself inspired by the trainers, the ways in which they connected with people," she says. "I got myself certified as a trainer, but I nevertheless continued to shadow some of the best trainers I knew, learning from all of them, absorbing their theories and practices. I loved the violin—still play—but this became an exciting new career."

She made the most of her mentoring and eventually became so popular—clients kept her busy fifteen hours a day—that she decided to "escape health-club burnout" and moved to Chicago. She married a violinist with the Chicago Symphony Orchestra and started training individual clients at various gyms. The word spread, and, after searching for a space to call her own for more than a year, she opened Grip Fitness in January.

It is a handsome, seventeen-hundred-square-foot facility just west of the Loop, filled with a few of the familiar contraptions one would find at the local gym, but with a minimalist feel. "This industry is moving very fast away from machines that are fastened to the floor," Queen says.

Off to the side, on a wall above a water fountain, a flat-screen monitor flashes inspirational quotations. They come from writers such as Anaïs Nin, and coaches and trainers, including Florida's Chuck Wolf: "The big empty room is the gym of the future."

"That goes to the whole ideal of what I am trying to do, to teach people that they might never need conventional gym equipment," she says. "I see exercise as a language of movement. I am always seeking ways to expand that vocabulary. I dream about exercises; at least twice a week, I wake up and put my new concepts down on a pad I keep next to the bed."

The doorbell rings, and Queen buzzes in her next client; she has about forty, and though she conducts group classes, she prefers one-on-one training. And so, here comes Max Eisenberg, a very fit-looking lawyer in his twenties who plays a lot of basketball at the East Bank Club. "I've had a lot of trainers," he says. "And I used to use a lot of machines. Here I don't, and I'm getting a much better workout."

They run through a few of Eisenberg's exercises and movements (as you can see from Osgood's photo). "What I am doing is creating a template for Max," Queen says. "The whole idea would be for him to not need me in a little while, to have learned enough to never need a trainer."

"That isn't great business sense, but..." Eisenberg says, smiling.

"I just can't train people who make me grumpy," Queen says.

MARCH 23, 2008

PUTTING A FACE ON WAR

Does anybody ride the "L" for any other reason than to get where they are going? Let us know. We don't expect a lot of responses. Though we have known a few people who who rode the "L" because they had no other place to sleep, or because the trains gave them packs of potential customers to whom they tried to sell everything from DVDs to dope to religion, we've yet to meet anyone who has said, "I ride the 'L' for fun." It's a necessary chore for most, and they bury themselves in a book or a newspaper, chat on the phone, close their eyes while listening to music, or pursue a nap. You rarely see people just staring out the windows: Been here, seen that.

So when conversations turn to "L" rides, they consist of complaints—justified because Chicago's transit system is an ongoing mess. But beleaguered as it is, it is still a wonder. Writers have taken note, as did Stuart Dybek in his short story "Pet Milk":

> We were speeding past scorched brick walls, gray windows, back porches outlined in sun, roofs, and treetops—the landscape of the 'L' I'd memorized from subway windows over a lifetime of rides: the podiatrist's foot sign past Fullerton; the bright pennants of Wrigley Field, at Addison; ancient hotels with TRANSIENTS WELCOME signs on their flaking brick walls; peeling and graffiti-smudged billboards; the old cemetery just before Wilson Avenue. Even without looking, I knew almost exactly where we were.

Riding the "L" can be an adventure, a chance to see the city from a side not highlighted in tourist brochures. From the trains and platforms you can see Chicago in intimate fashion and view some amazing things.

One of them is called the *Facade Project*, and it was begun in summer 2004, when artist Carrie Iverson started to fill the windows of the upper three floors of Chicago Printmakers Collaborative, 4642 North Western Avenue, with the faces of U.S. soldiers who had died in Iraq.

Some windows are visible from the street, but others are best seen from the Western Avenue platform of the Brown Line. There were 648 faces when the work was fully installed that summer, even then well short of the actual death toll (as of this writing, more than 3,300).

The faces generated some mild media interest that lasted about a second, and then faded into the fabric of the city. In 2006, Iverson created an installation titled *Wake* in the Phyllis Stigliano Gallery in Brooklyn that later moved to the Brooklyn Public Library. It was, she said, a continuation of the *Facade Project*, and it also included the faces of Iraqis killed. For those whose photos or names were not available, Iverson hauntingly chose to represent them with blank sheets of paper.

That is Iverson in the open window in Osgood's photo. She will continue to add to *Facade Project* and *Wake* until the troops return, which means, sadly, that you still have plenty of time to take a look.

MAY 6, 2007

WATT FUN IT IS

By now most of you have purchased and decorated (and by so doing actually created) your Christmas tree. It is likely you have also decorated your house or apartment. Maybe you've even decorated your lawn or your pet (antlers seem popular) or yourself, wandering around with one of those Santa Claus hats that we just saw hanging like moss from the ceiling at Walgreens and selling for $2.99 and $5.99.

Getting wilder with every year, Christmas decorating is a uniquely American folk art, and like all art forms, has its critics and its fans, with the critics bemoaning the increasingly flashy extravagance and schizophrenic imagery of it all—Santa Claus sitting with Baby Jesus (and maybe even Elvis); reindeer, elves, and pink flamingos keeping company—as another example of the crass commercialization of the holidays.

Chicago gallery owner Aron Packer, an expert in folk art, once told me, "If you give twenty people the same ten Santas and the same ten reindeer and the same amount of lighting, they will all create something different, and perhaps two would qualify, for me, as art.

"But America being America, we naturally infuse the old with the new. And the results are a cross between the secular and the religious, between the New Testament and Disney World. But I have as much respect for the people who decorate their homes for the holidays as I do for Monet."

Walking around Daley Plaza and the massive tree there, it was hard not to appreciate its beauty while at the same time being overwhelmed.

So we left the plaza and, walking north along Clark Street, stopped at the river. There we remembered a story and tried to imagine what it must have been like to be in the crowds along the dock in those long-ago Novembers, starting in the 1880s, when ships would arrive loaded with evergreens brought from the North. These vessels, these Christmas ships, did a lucrative business; trees that were purchased for two cents in the Upper Peninsula of Michigan could be sold for as much as seventy-five cents here.

Heading east to Michigan Avenue, we remembered the story of a couple of clever designers named Joe Kreis and George Silvestri, who in 1959 forever changed the way Chicago would look at Christmas when they put strings of delicate lights that Silvestri had found in Italy through the six barren elm trees in front of the bygone Saks Fifth Avenue store at Michigan Avenue and Erie Street.

Then came the Water Tower and its tiny park. The trees were surprisingly bare, but it was otherwise bejeweled by two canopies of lights and more in the shape of a fountain, and on the corner was a horse attached to a carriage and wearing one of those Santa hats (extra large?) and bells around its neck, jingling so softly that their sound could barely be heard amid the rush of traffic and the happy human chatter.

DECEMBER 30, 2007

FIELD OF BAD DREAMS

They are sad reminders of the perils of the road, those makeshift memorials that pop up after fatal crashes. They take many forms—flowers, candles, and crosses, mostly—but they are not always what they seem. A few weeks ago, driving along Route 71 near the Illinois towns of Ottawa and Norway, we came upon the large item in Osgood's photo and immediately thought it the site of a tragic airplane accident. No one was around to ask, but there was a plaque near the plane:

DEDICATED TO . . . ALL FARMERS AND AG-RELATED BUSINESS FOLKS THAT HAVE LIVED THROUGH THE 'AGRICULTURAL CRASH' OF THE 1980s.

Eventually, we unraveled the mystery.

The 1940s-era twin-engine aircraft and the plaque were put there by Merv and Phyllis Eastwold, the husband and wife who own nearby Norwegian Implement Co. Indeed, there is another sign (an advertisement, if you will) on the site, directing people to that firm, "Illinois' Largest Stihl Dealer" (for you urbanites, Stihl is a major manufacturer of portable power tools).

"[But] nobody ever sees that sign, because they're busy gawking at the plane," said Craig Wieczorkiewicz, the Streator bureau chief for the *Times* newspaper in Ottawa and a man wise in the history of the area.

The mangled plane was originally on the property of a resort in Arkansas and was later sold to Merv's brother John. When he failed to get permission to install it in a lake near his home, it made its way here.

It is a sad memorial, a reminder of those years not so long past (the first Farm Aid concert was in 1985) when family farms were dying in vast numbers. And it certainly is an eye-catcher.

More subtle, but also important, is the nearby Illinois Norwegian Settlers State Memorial, commemorating the 1834 founding of Norway, the first permanent Norwegian settlement in the U.S. Born the year after Chicago was incorporated as a town, Norway came to be known as "the mother settlement," for it was the jumping-off point for immigrants who spread their farming skills throughout the Midwest.

The town of Norway isn't much now, just a speck on the map. But on June 23, 1934, the day the state memorial was dedicated, and less than a week after Merv Eastwold moved to the area, more than ten thousand people showed up for the ceremony, and almost all of them were farmers.

JUNE 24, 2007

PASTRAMI AND POLITICS

One recent morning, Osgood and I were relieved to walk into Manny's Coffee Shop & Deli and not find any political candidates or their spouses. I told Osgood that I remembered being in the place on the morning Maggie Daley, during her husband's successful run for mayor in 1989, teased reporters by playfully asking, "Do I have corned beef between my teeth?"

Once the election season starts to heat up later this year, Manny's will be, once again, a stop on the campaign trail. It is one of the places candidates—some of whom have never been here before—meet "regular folks" and "take the pulse" of the city.

This place—Lou Mitchell's, just west of the Loop, is another—is also a favorite of television news crews that visit when their bosses are eager for an early morning reaction of the "regular folks" to current events.

"It's easier to interview people who are sitting down and eating eggs," a veteran TV newshound once explained.

Some of the Manny's regulars have been on TV often enough that they should be paying AFTRA dues. Most of them just want to be left alone, to eat in peace or argue with their rumpled and opinionated pals.

Manny's is a great place, a Chicago classic lacking in pretense and filled with all sorts of hearty foods and good conversation.

On a recent visit, we ran into a couple enjoying corned beef sandwiches.

Jim Blake and Betsy Samuels said they were visiting from California and had found Manny's through a Zagat guidebook.

"They said it was the closest thing Chicago has to a New York deli," said Blake.

"Food's great," said Samuels.

The conversation turned to politics. We mentioned Manny's election-time star status.

"So, what you're saying is that this would be a good place for Gov. Schwarzenegger to stop, in a few years, when he's running for president?" Blake asked, without a trace of playfulness in his voice.

Sᴇᴘᴛᴇᴍʙᴇʀ 7, 2003

SCREEN SAVERS

Being in a rather silly mood, and fully believing it likely that the junior U.S. senator from New York once watched movies at the Pickwick Theatre, I suggested to Osgood that she had occupied the very seat in which I was sitting. "Maybe she even held hands with a boyfriend," Osgood said, and I could not—would not, actually—disagree.

Hillary Clinton is a child of Park Ridge, and it is inconceivable that any child of this northwest suburb did not visit this most majestic of movie palaces.

When the Pickwick opened in 1928, it served, as was customary at the time, as both movie house and vaudeville theater. It was less than two decades after the city was incorporated (with only two thousand residents), and it is fun to consider what a pleasant furor the opening caused.

Imagine how gaga the first patrons, there to watch the film *Wings*, must have been seeing the

building, with its one-hundred-foot tower topped with a flashing iron lantern, and entering the 1,424-seat auditorium featuring bold, geometric Art Deco-ish designs of obvious Aztec and Mayan inspiration.

Architects Roscoe Harold Zook and William F. McCaughey, both students of Frank Lloyd Wright, created an eye-catching gem, aided by the lobby-work of sculptor Alfonso Iannelli.

That was the way movie theaters were made in those days, nowhere more so than in Chicago. In the book *The Best Remaining Seats: The Golden Age of the Movie Palace*, author Ben Hall characterizes Chicago in the 1920s as "the jumpingest movie city in the world [with] more plush, elegant theaters than anywhere else."

It is sad to contemplate and catalog the departed: Tivoli, Norshore, Marbro, Paradise, Diversey, Apollo...enough.

The Pickwick has survived, thrived, and even attained a quiet stardom; it was, for years, featured as the backdrop for the opening of Gene Siskel and Roger Ebert's TV show *At the Movies*.

The theater was named to the National Register of Historic Places in 1975, and in 1990, three smaller theaters were added, without diminishing the size of the main auditorium.

In 1999, the Pickwick Preservation Council was formed to explore ways to use the theater for concerts, plays, and other events. Last fall it began a "Pickwick Live" series that included productions by the Organic Theater Company, musical events, and children's theater. The palace is often packed with little boys and girls, blissfully years away from careers and politics.

MAY 20, 2001

MIDNIGHT MAESTRO

There is only one Buddy Charles, and there he was one night, or early morning, telling me, "I would walk down Randolph Street when it was crowded with clubs and just soak in all the music....So many wonderful sounds just pouring out into the night." It is impossible to calculate the number of nights and early mornings I sat near Buddy Charles and listened to him talk and sing and play the piano. Too young to have caught him at such bygone clubs as the Blue Note, Jazz Limited, the Casino, the Riptide, Curly's Show Lounge, or the Playroom, I was a frequent visitor during the eighteen years he held late-night court at the Acorn on Oak, and later, in the more rarefied Coq d'Or in the Drake Hotel.

It was there one night, or early morning, that he told me, "I have not one regret. If they nailed me in the box tomorrow, I could go knowing I got away with everything. I fooled 'em all."

He is a living encyclopedia of American music. As my colleague, Howard Reich, has written, "Listen to an hour of Charles' piano and you'll hear a virtual history of jazz and pop keyboard playing of the twentieth century."

He started early: "I can remember as a child sitting under the piano as my mother [Ruth] played, and my hands just kept moving, my tiny fingers flying through the air."

He began taking lessons in the sixth grade, and quit for a while after joining the Mt. Carmel High School boxing team and serving for two years in the Army. He started playing again at Loyola University, where he majored in what might be the perfect subjects for a career as a piano man, philosophy and psychology. He toyed with the idea of teaching, but there were so many clubs then, eager for a talented and tireless performer.

Fats Waller was a big influence on his playing, as was jazz great Muggsy Spanier, Charles' stepfather: "I was there when they met. At Jazz Limited, Muggsy accidentally on purpose knocked my mom's coat on the floor, brushed it off, and in a flash, there I was, the best man at their wedding."

Charles is married to Pat, who abandoned a successful New York stage career to marry him more than fifty years ago and who told me, "He is the only man I ever met who I knew I could spend my life with. I have never missed the theater. My life with Buddy and the kids allowed me to discover other facets of life. I've had the best of it all. All thanks to this lovely man."

He is devoted to Pat. But there are hundreds, perhaps thousands, of others who have had satisfying relationships with Charles. Whether these lasted for just an hour or have continued through the decades (he still plays now and then at Chambers in Niles), he has never let us down.

He knows the secret, and he put it poetically one long-ago night, or early morning, when he leaned across the keys of his piano and said, "There is something primitive about being close to live music. What makes it work is that people are inherently eager for intimacy."

JULY 27, 2008

PETS ROCK

For years, I was a judge at the Halloween pet costume contests held at the bygone Parkview Pet Store. I saw cats dressed as clowns and old women. I met a little boy who dressed (I was afraid to ask him how) a bird no bigger than a hand in a Dracula costume.

I saw a couple of tiny dogs dressed as ballerinas and two large Labs decked out as gangsters. One dog, painted green and in a box, was a Chia Pet. During these events I would wonder whether some pet owners were in need of psychiatric help.

It's not news that people are nuts about their pets, and no one has tapped into this condition more successfully than Janice Brown. "It started when my husband came home with a stray dog," she said. "I became frustrated by the difficulties I was having getting information from various groups and agencies. And in spending time with our dog and other dog owners, I really started to understand how deep the relationship is between people and their pets. I started to think that there should be a way to create a bridge between the animal-welfare community and pet owners."

In 2000, her passion took form in the magazine *Chicagoland Tails*. The first printing was fifteen thousand copies. It has since grown into a national publishing empire called Tails Pet Media Group, Inc. Now more than 675,000 copies are hitting stores eleven times a year here and in twelve other major markets, such as St. Louis, Indianapolis, Philadelphia, and New Jersey.

It's a handsome publication; about 25 percent of each issue is tailored for different markets. It has book and product reviews, feature stories, and serious articles.

"This magazine definitely fills a niche for the Chicago-area pet owner in terms of providing information about products and services," said Jennifer Boznos, owner of Call of the Wild, a North Side training facility and day-care center for dogs. "The staff and I especially enjoy the magazine's 'Best Of' year-end polls."

The magazine has a lot of ads. "We never charge not-for-profits," said Brown's father, Alan. "And no ads for puppy mills or breeders."

As are most fathers, Brown is proud of his daughter (and the other two he has). A couple of years ago, when she came to him for advice, he became "intrigued by the absence of a national pet magazine, and also by the fact that pet advertising is a $42 billion market." He was so intrigued, in fact, that this year he sold his successful audio-visual communications business to his employees and became the executive publisher of Tails Pet Media Group. "I feel lucky to be working with him," said Janice Brown. "It's kind of the reverse of the traditional family business."

That's Brown with other members of her family—husband Barry Gork and kids Liv, five, Mallory, three, and Avery, one—on the floor in her office. The serious-looking character to the left is Luna. She's eight.

DECEMBER 2, 2007

MAXWELL STREET BLUES

Some years ago Osgood and I stood on the northeast corner of Halsted and Maxwell Streets and listened to a man named Bobby Davis sing the blues and play the guitar. The street was dying. As I wrote then, "The curbs are broken, the sidewalks smashed and thrown askew as if by a small earthquake. It's a shattered, tattered, and shuttered street."

The University of Illinois at Chicago, which owned much of the land in the area and was in need of expanding its campus, was moving in for the kill.

A group of concerned citizens, activists, and blues performers had formed the Maxwell Street Historic Preservation Coalition in an attempt to save something of the street. They had created on the corner a sculpture that spelled M-A-X in ten-foot-tall letters made of railroad ties, and the *Maxwell Street Wall of Fame*, a mural filled with names of former area residents, such as bluesman Bo Diddley, jazzman Benny Goodman, and former Supreme Court Justice Arthur Goldberg.

Near the mural was a cardboard petition. Only five names and addresses were scrawled on it.

It was obviously a losing battle, but I asked then, "Are there not ways to save a slice of Maxwell Street, to memorialize its significance, its soul?"

There were many other voices calling for salvation.

Ira Berkow, a native Chicagoan and former *New York Times* sportswriter, wrote a wonderful history titled *Maxwell Street: Survival in a Bazaar* in 1977. In a speech decades later, he called Maxwell Street "the Ellis Island of the Midwest" and passionately pleaded against its "annihilation." To those listening, there was evoked what was: the voices of thousands of immigrants hawking their wares and dreaming their dreams of success in a frenzied zoo of a marketplace, where almost anything was for sale and the air was thick with aspirations.

Having been a frequent early Sunday morning visitor to the original Maxwell Street market, sometimes following the philosophy that the best way to cure a hangover was to eat a Polish sausage and to haggle for twenty minutes over the price of a dozen pairs of socks, I was sad to see it vanish, almost as if it was being erased anew every week, and never did warm up to the "new" Maxwell Street market that started taking up Sunday space on Canal Street between Taylor and Sixteenth Streets in 1994, when the university made clear its plans to expand into the old market area.

It held on for a bit and the new Sunday setting attracted an altogether "cleaner" breed of crowd and vendors. The idea for it, expressed some years ago by Constance Buscemi, director of the city's

Department of Consumer Services, was to "take everything that was positive from the old market minus the crime, the dirtiness, the people hawking pornographic videos" and to create a place where one could "see more families than ever before."

The old market was never family-friendly, though it was grand and funky fun. And one Sunday, the new market was filled with families. A couple of blues musicians enlivened the morning air with their music, but the whole scene, though not without some appeal, more resembled a suburban flea market than the original's charming chaos.

I'd like to think that some of the people there were sharing stories of the old market, as they might talk of Riverview while visiting Great America. Memories are all many of us will have.

Though conservationists fought hard to preserve some vestige, some living sign of what was once the Maxwell Street market amidst the university's $525 million expansion, demolition crews razed the buildings on the street. And memories were to be found only in the dust and debris.

And now, where we once listened to Bobby Davis sing the blues there stood a new building, its windowed ground-floor space advertising for a tenant that could join the trio of gentrified neighbors sitting on the other corners: Jamba Juice, Caribou Coffee, and a TV-filled sports bar called Morgan's on Maxwell.

There is nothing wrong with change. A city is an organic thing. But when change eradicates important and vibrant parts of the past, a city becomes less alive.

There is a plaque on one building:

SITE OF THE ORIGINAL MAXWELL STREET MARKET—CIRCA 1890

and some small informational stands, offering the most perfunctory history lessons, spaced along the chic, shop-filled block east of Halsted.

There are also three sculptures: a woman carrying a sack of groceries; a man presumably trying to sell tomatoes; and the statue in Osgood's photo, a man playing the guitar. Produced by a company in Pennsylvania, these statues are not ugly. They are, in what they have to say about the price of progress, pathetic.

PLAY'S THE THING

When sunlight pours through the tall windows on the ground floor of the building at Twenty-third Street and Michigan Avenue, it is not hard to imagine how seductively such light played off the paint and chrome of the cars that sat in here when this was an auto dealership. We are in the South Loop, a neighborhood rich in history; among the less-savory elements of its past were a nightclub, the Four Deuces, and a couple of hotels, the Metropole and Lexington, all favorites of Al Capone. It is now so alive with fresh construction and loft conversions that it seems as up-to-the-minute and history-free as a housing development in Huntley.

More than a year ago, two women looked at this corner and saw their future. Josephine Sanders, a former IT consultant and the mother of six-year-old twin boys, and Sherri Murphy, once a flight attendant and the mother of a three-year-old son, had become friends after bumping into one another at various North Side kid-play emporiums, to which they had schlepped from their homes in South Shore and Bronzeville, respectively. The two started brainstorming, and now, after borrowing money and advice, they have Room2Play. It's impossible to miss at 2255 South Michigan Avenue, open from 9:30 AM to 5:30 PM weekdays, 9:30 AM to noon on weekends. It's twelve dollars per day, per kid, with six-month and annual memberships available.

It is not a day-care center. Parents or caretakers (who get in free) arrive with their tiny visitors and they stay, most of them watching the children as they also read books or newspapers. A few get involved, becoming tea-party guests, slayers of monsters, outer-space creatures, or one of the other infinite creations that seem so easily to leap to life from a child's mind.

There's more than enough room for them all, more than four-thousand carpeted square feet, with a colorful wall mural and toys, clothes, books, blocks, plastic food, balls, stuffed animals, and other playthings. Geared for kids up to ages seven or eight, it is purposefully low-tech.

"We want to foster interactive play," says Sanders.

The first year has been encouraging for the two owner-managers. Word of mouth has been good, and there have been an increasing number of private parties as well as new classes and events. Osgood was there for the facility's first concert, in late March, which featured Ella Jenkins before a packed house (that's Murphy and Sanders, left to right, in Osgood's photo).

"We aren't sure what to expect during our first summer," says Murphy. "In the winter, people came because they were going stir-crazy."

As Murphy began to explain the details of the ambitious summer-camp program that begins later this month, Osgood thought about taking more pictures. But then a little girl making a cake with a little boy invited us to a dinner party, and we just couldn't say no.

JUNE 1, 2008

SHOW BUSINESS

The walls of the law offices of Jay Ross are, as you can see in Osgood's photo, covered with pictures. These are some, just some, of the collages and what Ross calls "assemblages" that the entertainment lawyer has spent much of his life accumulating. "I do this instead of going to a shrink," he says. The frames contain photos, autographs, letters, and other memorabilia of, in an aggressively eclectic gathering, such famous people as William Faulkner, Malcolm X, Albert Schweitzer, Igor Stravinsky, Neil Armstrong, Anne Frank, Sammy Davis Jr., Mahatma Gandhi, and James Brown, who was a longtime client.

"He always treated me with respect," Ross says.

In certain circles, Ross, sixty-six, is as famous as many of those on his walls (and in the thick binders in which he keeps more photos and autographs).

He was born in Brooklyn, and after his parents died when he was two, he was raised in Rockford by an uncle who was in the roofing/siding business. He earned a degree from the University of Illinois College of Law in 1967 and eventually started practicing in Chicago.

He had worked his way through college and law school booking bands for concerts, so he was well-known on the music scene. That's why Muddy Waters came to see him about a problem with an insurance company. "He thought I did a good job, so he passed my name to some of his friends," Ross says.

Those friends were performers such as Willie Dixon, Albert King, T-Bone Walker, Pop Staples, Dinah Washington—an endless parade of entertainers that continues.

"Most of the work I did involved going after the people who weren't paying my clients royalties," he recalls, then adds dryly, "Every record company's finances—you ever hear of a mistake in favor of the artist?"

For thirty years he has been tenacious in "getting the artists what they deserve." He has also found time to host a radio show (*The Rappin' Lawyer*), TV show (*Jay B. Ross Backstage Pass*), lecture, and teach. A decade ago, he was named to a couple of *New City* magazine's lists of the most influential people in the local music scene, and this year he received a Lifetime Achievement Award at the Chicago Music Awards, the only nonmusician so honored.

"I am low profile because I stay in Chicago," Ross says. "I still go out, but I'm older now, and I'm trying not to kill myself. If I'm out late listening to music, I come to work late the next day."

Unmarried ("Music has been my mistress."), Ross lives on the North Side and still works every day in offices that sit in an unglamorous part of town, west of the river. "What I really wanted to be was an actor," he says, "but I was afraid I'd starve."

APRIL 6, 2008

THE LEVEL'S ADVOCATE

I f you were to ask a thousand Chicagoans this question, "How many feet above sea level is Chicago?" how many correct answers do you think you'd get? Our guess is zero.

People would be more likely to know Ernie Banks' career home run total (512) or Oprah Winfrey's middle name (Gail). The same is not true in Woodstock. As you can see from Osgood's photo of the town's courthouse, Woodstock is, or was, more than a century ago, 954 feet above sea level. This fact was important enough for architect John Mills Van Osdel, or one of those who commissioned the building in 1857, to loudly note it in stone (the opposite side of the entrance carries an even more esoteric fact: The town is, or was, 373 feet above Lake Michigan).

"Such a thing is not unique," says Tim Samuelson, cultural historian for the City of Chicago. "But perhaps such facts were just more important to people back then."

The courthouse was built to resemble the 1853 Cook County Courthouse (Van Osdel was noted for being earnestly derivative), which was destroyed in the Chicago Fire of 1871. The adjoining structure, the Sheriff's House and Jail, was built in 1887, and its most famous guest was labor organizer Eugene Debs, held there awaiting trial for his part in the Pullman Strike of 1894.

Over the decades, the two buildings fell into very sad shape, and by 1972 they were threatened with being torn down to make room for a parking lot. Saved by locals Cliff and Bev Ganschow, the buildings came back to renovated life and were later listed on the National Register of Historic Places. They now contain, among many pleasant surprises, a couple of nice restaurants, an art gallery, a pottery shop, offices, and the Chester Gould–Dick Tracy Museum, Gould having called Woodstock home for a half-century.

The little boy sitting on the stairs is Andrew Gippert, who says he loves the courthouse, as well as basketball, reading, and writing. He has just entered second grade but has, as did others in his first-grade class for an assignment at Westwood Elementary School, already written his first novel. It is called *The Robot Who Played Basketball*, and perhaps he is on his way to following in the creative footsteps of Orson Welles, who grew up here but did not, as far as we know, write anything in first grade.

But it is something to know that Welles walked these very streets and saw some of the buildings. History here is appreciated more than in most places, and you will find people eager to debate which is the gem of the town square, the courthouse or the nearby Opera House, built in 1889 and still a vibrant venue. They are lively discussions, but beside the point. This tiny town is filled with buildings that bring the past to the present.

And so how many feet above sea level is Chicago? The answer is 578.5, according to the Chicago Public Library, the next time you're looking to win a bar bet.

SEPTEMBER 23, 2007

FRIENDLY WRITERS

I just got an e-mail. I am, like many of you, always just getting an e-mail. They arrive at a steady pace, and the one that I just got is, like most of them, a meaningless missive. Even those from friends lack the warmth that comes from the effort used to put pen to paper. It's an icy form of communication, but that's what we've got to live with, at least until e-mail is made old-fashioned by whatever comes next down the cyberspace trail.

One way to fully appreciate how we used to communicate is to travel back to January 1, 1906. And so, you are standing in the home of Frances and John Jacob Glessner at Eighteenth Street and Prairie Avenue. You are there for the meeting of the Monday morning reading group.

Friday- July- 27-1906

John Calvert Donaldson   Julie Vary Donaldson   Norman Vary Donaldson

Mrs. Glessner is presented with a gift to celebrate her fifty-eighth birthday. It is a twelve-by-eighteen-inch, four-inch-thick, handmade book, and you watch the surprise and delight on Mrs. Glessner's face as she turns its pages, each of them marking one of the days of the year, and each containing a message of the most personal and artful sort.

Thanks to the diligent efforts of William Tyre, of the Society of Architectural Historians, this book has been brought back to life and is on exhibit in the Glessner House Museum, 1800 South Prairie Avenue.

It is under glass, too fragile to have people flipping through its pages—see how carefully the begloved Corina Carusi, the museum's director and curator, is handling it in Osgood's photo—but Tyre has photographed more than one hundred of the book's pages and researched every one of the contributors, and his work constitutes the meat of the exhibit.

It is a fascinating, even enchanting, look at the way we were.

The contributors are neighbors and friends, some quite famous: architect Daniel Burnham; Theodore Thomas, the founder and first conductor of the Chicago Symphony Orchestra, and his second wife, Fay, who founded the Anti-Cruelty Society; William Rainey Harper, the first president of the University of Chicago (who, for reasons unknown, is the only person to have been given two pages); Frederick Law Olmsted, the landscaping genius.

The pages contain photos, poems, musical notes, messages of all sorts gathered by Elizabeth Johnson, one of the members of Mrs. Glessner's Monday reading group. One looks at them and marvels at the thought and time and effort that went into the making.

Oh, well…:-)

FEBRUARY 18, 2007

FREEDOM FRYERS

As a rule and almost as a religion, Osgood and I avoid fast-food chains. But we are kind of nuts for Harold's, more formally Harold's Chicken Shack or The Fried Chicken King. This is a chain in name only because each of its outlets is distinctive. In the definitive history of the operation, headlined "The First Family of Fried Chicken" in the April 14, 2006, edition of the *Chicago Reader*, writer Mike Sula called the chain "a confederacy of individual outlets."

It was started in 1950 by an African-American named Harold Pierce, an entrepreneurial native of Alabama. His first fried chicken restaurant, at Forty-seventh Street and Greenwood Avenue, was a huge success, and in time he franchised his name and secret recipe, and shacks began to pop up in converted spaces across the South Side. He had no competition from fast-food chains because, at the time, they ignored African-American neighborhoods. Pierce was not a hands-on homogenizer, and as a result, many of the other shack owners messed with the tasty template. They speeded up the cooking process (originally the chicken wasn't fried until ordered, which meant a fifteen-minute wait), varied the sauces and seasonings, and offered new menu items. No store looked like any other store, running the gamut from seedy to sparkling.

There are about seventy Harold's places now, most of them here and a few in other cities, and each has a number attached to its name. One woman we recently met told us, "I have been searching for Number 1 for years. Surely you and Osgood have seen it. Tell me where it is!"

We could not, and here's a reason why, as Sula reported in his story: "The original Number 1, Harold's first shack, is long gone; the current Number 1, at 7139 South State Street, used to be Number 6, though it appears to have closed last week. Number 92 is in Milwaukee, Number 94 in Minneapolis, but there's no longer a Number 93. For that matter there's no longer a 16, 42, 43, 44, 45, or 78, though there could be again someday."

Got that?

The Harold's in Osgood's photo is new, opened in November by Tracey and Greg Edingburg. (That's Tracey with cook Ken Goddar in Osgood's photo.) It is at 11322 South Michigan Avenue, and Edingburg, a Chicago firefighter, says he opened it to try to give something back to the community. On the wall is a calming pastoral mural, and the place is Number 11, in honor of the first fire truck of Edingburg's career.

Including Number 11, we have now eaten at, if memory serves, six Harold's. Sula, brave man that he is, ate at thirty-five in one year, concluding that "it's near impossible to predict which ones fry good chicken." Still, if you are driving around and spot a Harold's, give it a try. Each is, in a real way, a Chicago original.

APRIL 15, 2007

BRONZING THE MESSENGER

A bronze statue of Irv Kupcinet seems to be enjoying its first winter in Chicago, standing in the middle of the sidewalk near the northeast corner of Wacker Drive and Wabash Avenue, just steps from the bridge that also bears his name. There is a *Chicago Sun-Times* tucked under his right arm, and a smile on his face.

A layer of snow across his shoulders looks, for a far-fetched moment, like the pads he wore when he was a quarterback for the University of North Dakota. That was before he would spend sixty years—mostly in print, but also on local TV and radio—chronicling the comings and goings, deals, and witticisms of celebrities, power brokers, and characters, giving them all a bit of bold-faced, if fleeting, fame.

The Kup statue is a new member of a select club of immortalized immortals. It joins several hundred other statues around the city. Most are of poets, soldiers, and statesmen; almost all of them are of men. Kup, as far as we know, is the only newspaperman to be so honored, here or in any other city.

You can argue—and bring into the mix the statues of sportscasters Harry Caray and Jack Brickhouse if you like—that Kup is not as deserving as Columbus, Shakespeare, Ben Franklin, Goethe, or any of the others who have statues here. But Kup will be standing where he is long after we vanish. And we will vanish for keeps unless we have family and friends with the clout, dough, and desire to resurrect us in bronze or marble or steel.

When Kup turned ninety in 2002, there was a party at the Palmer House Hilton. Hundreds of guests heard WGN radio's Wally Phillips say, "Kup isn't a piece of Chicago. He is Chicago and always will be."

Kup died the next year, and now he is a piece of Chicago, a nine-foot-tall bronze piece standing on a pedestal. It is the work of Preston Jackson, a professor of sculpture at the School of the Art Institute. The statue was unveiled July 31, on what would have been the columnist's ninety-fourth birthday. And that should have been that: a few tears, some kind words, and then leave the statue to its mute and frozen life.

But this summer, on what would be his ninety-fifth birthday, a part of Kup, his Purple Heart Cruise, will be reborn. He started these one-day lake cruises in 1945 as a way to honor wounded and elderly veterans. The trips ended in 1995, after treating more than thirty-five thousand vets to a day of diversions. They stopped because Kup had gotten old and frail and, frankly, the vets were dying off. But now there are more wars being fought and, tragically, disabled vets aplenty, and so Kup's grandson, David, and some pals were inspired to relaunch the cruise.

Yes, Kup is just a statue now, and in life he was just a newspaperman. But what has Goethe done for us lately?

FEBRUARY 11, 2007

MAN OF A THOUSAND PHASES

There are many ways to age, and many words to describe the process. But to say that Alan Barcus is aging gracefully—a good word with which most of us would be happy—doesn't come close to capturing the vibrancy of this seventy-year-old's life. Looking twenty years younger than the calendar would have it, Barcus has just released his second CD, a wonderfully eclectic package titled *Don't I Know*. He did so with an October party at the Acorn Theater in Three Oaks, Michigan, where Osgood captured him at the piano. "About time for my second CD. Thirty years between releases," he says, flashing the area's most self-effacing smile.

Barcus attended Indiana State University, where he was a star athlete and received a master's degree in business. He started a jazz trio and coached sports for a time, and then, with wife, Ann, and young daughter, Katie, and no job, came to Chicago in the late 1960s. He soon was leading the orchestra at the Playboy Club and was musical director of the play *Hair*, where he met and formed a lifelong friendship with a young Chicago actor named Joe Mantegna.

In the early 1970s he and Mantegna wrote a musical. Mantegna went off to become a movie star, and Barcus became a prolific and successful composer, lyricist, arranger, songwriter, playwright, and pianist. He has composed for film. His songs have been performed by such artists as Peggy Lee.

Go to Cubs games? You have heard his "You're My Cubs," the official team fight song.

Watch TV or listen to radio? Then you have heard some of his more than twenty-four hundred commercials, for such big clients as McDonald's, United Airlines, Kellogg's, and Pepsi. That is his voice, singing his words, on the can't-get-it-out-of-your-head jingle for Car-X: "Rattle rattle, thunder clatter, boom, boom, boom…"

In addition to his artistic accomplishments, he is one of the greatest gray-haired basketball players in the world. He played for the Chicago Masters Basketball team, national champions in 2001, 2002, and 2004, and was twice most valuable player. In the International Games, he was a member of the gold-medal Team USA in Helsinki in 1998, and again in Hamburg in 2006.

Barcus sings most of the songs on the new CD, which include the work of such talented musical friends as Dick Noel, Orville Stoeber, Matt Burden, Leah Banicki, and Gary Pigg.

One song, "It Ain't Easy Gettin' Old," contains the words, "One time when you were hot, you said, 'What happens when you're not?'"

That is not a question Barcus will likely have to answer for some time, if ever.

JANUARY 14, 2007

WHEN AN UNLOVELY FLAME DIES

Happy New Year to you nearly three-million citizens of the great state of Illinois who, on January 1, will no longer be smoking in restaurants, bars, nightclubs, workplaces, and all public buildings because of Public Act 095-0017, also know as the Smoke Free Illinois Act. Many, many people say they are going to try to quit smoking, attempt to join those ten million or so nonsmoking Illinoisans, save a few bucks, maybe add some years to their lives. But there are rebels, among them the members of the University Club Cigar Society, some of whom can be seen in Osgood's photo enjoying what they enjoy at a recent gathering of the group.

"Although the law is going to drive us a bit underground, we will continue to meet twice a month but I cannot say where," declares the society's secretary, Curtis Tuckey.

If you have never smoked, you cannot imagine the anxiety and nostalgia that have clouded the final days of smoke-filled rooms.

One such place, smoke-chocked for more than four decades, plans to go gently into the new fresh-air age. "We'll just put all the ashtrays away," said Billy Goat bartender Jeff Magill.

But some of those along the bar were smoking and recalling a time, not so very long ago, when people smoked everywhere.

"There were ashtrays on the tennis courts at my health club," said one of a threesome of smokers, all over fifty.

"You could smoke in elevators, hospitals, banks," said another.

"And in cabs, on the 'L,' on airplanes," said the third.

One smoker recalled that once, people quit smoking by, well, quitting smoking.

"No nicotine-laced gum, nicotine patches, hypnosis, or acupuncture," said one of the smokers.

"No support groups or sitting down with a shrink," said another.

"That's the way I'm going to do it," said another. "For so long I've been made to feel like an outcast, I'm going cold turkey just to prove I'm no weakling. Think I can do it?"

People have long known the dangers of smoking, and most of those who do so—or who eat double bacon cheeseburgers for breakfast, drown themselves in booze, or participate in unsafe sex—know they will have to pay the price.

"I just don't like being told what to do," said one of the smokers.

"How about another drink?" someone asked.

The answers were quick.

"Sure."

"Love one."

"Why not?"

DECEMBER 30, 2007

FACE TO FACE

It is impossible to imagine a more devoted visual artist than James Kuhn, who has spent the last year turning himself into art. It began when he was snowed in one night at his house in Michigan. He painted his face, took a photo of it, posted the photo on Flickr, got some positive reaction, and then set out on a 365-day adventure that ended earlier this month. "He is an artist in every sense of the word," says David Fink, a friend who co-owns the Acorn Theater in Three Oaks, Michigan. "He has truly original ideas. Not only does he think of these incredible artistic transformations, but he has the ability to execute them brilliantly. Only photos and short videos remain to document the sometimes playful, sometimes disturbing, but always unique works of art he has created."

Indeed. As powerfully as Osgood's photo captures one day in the life of Kuhn's face, it is necessary to employ modern technologies to understand and appreciate the scope and inventiveness of what he is doing. And so, a visit to the Internet (hawhawjames.livejournal.com) will provide a tour through a "gallery" (there is video too; go to youtube.com, and search for "James Kuhn") that is amusing, spooky, thought-provoking, wistful, philosophical, and mesmerizing, as a human face vanishes into...well, whatever his imagination conjures and paint allows.

Most of the time, the creation is seen in the flesh, so to speak, only by Kuhn. But he sometimes parades the canvas/face out and about, and he has discovered that "face art has opened doors for me into a new acceptance....Suddenly I am beset by people who would ordinarily not give me the time of day."

Kim Clark, Fink's partner in life and the Acorn, has known Kuhn for a long time and says, "There are no limits to his imagination. As a prodigy at the Art Institute, where Kuhn received his bachelor's degree in painting and drawing, he often would show up desperately late for class because his time and energy was invested in creating elaborate creations that he wore around the city all day—a caped figure with wild top hats or angel wings wandering down Michigan Avenue.

"A painting sits on a wall and does not move, but when you put art on a person, they move. And many, many more people see your work."

We did not bother Kuhn in his project's final weeks, reluctant to disturb what he calls "the solitude and quiet of this personal experience."

But he's already thinking about what might come next and writes that he "cannot see ever running out of inspiration for this art form. Skin is so interesting!"

He started his unique journey knowing that he could never "sell a painting that is painted on my own flesh." That may seem crazy to some. It's admirable to us.

APRIL 19, 2009

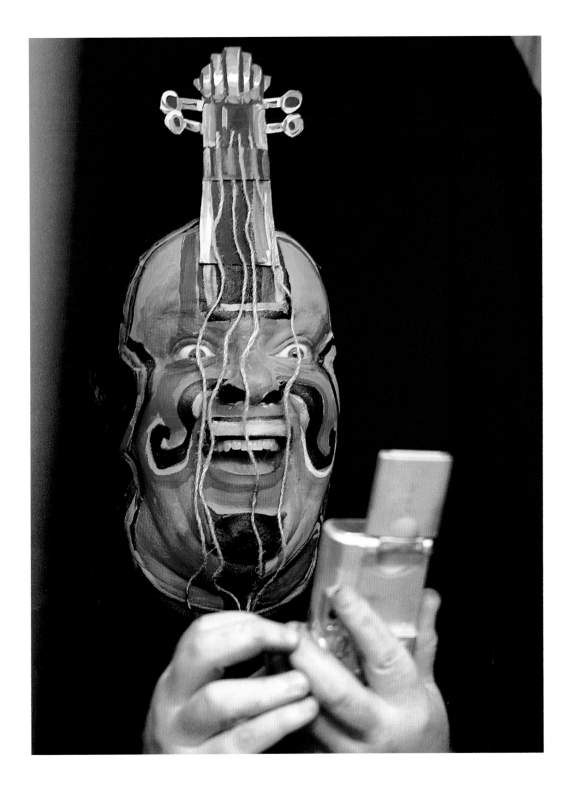

JOHN PAUL'S JONES

February is a cold month, and so it was last year, brutally so, on the day Barack Obama stood in Springfield and announced his candidacy for president. Whether or not U.S. voters elect another Illinoisan as chief executive this fall, it's a comfort to know that the one we've already produced is the most popular ever. Popular with writers, that is, for it is impossible to calculate the number of books that have been written about Abraham Lincoln; many thousands, certainly.

A recent *Time* magazine article calmly asserted that there have been "more books written about Lincoln than any other American," and a critic, reviewing 2002's *Lincoln's Virtues: An Ethical Biography* in the *New York Times*, wrote that "more words have been written about Abraham Lincoln than any historical personage except Jesus Christ."

More books join the shelves every month. Last month—Lincoln's birthday month—gave us, among many new offerings, *Douglass and Lincoln*, about Lincoln's relationship with African-American leader Frederick Douglass, and *Lincoln and Douglas*, about his debates with rival politician Stephen A. Douglas.

The Lincoln section of Prairie Archives, a marvelously messy and altogether wonderful bookstore in Springfield, contains five hundred titles. "I'd say that's the number, though it is always changing," says John Paul, who, fresh out of graduate school, started Prairie Archives in 1971 as a mail-order operation.

"I never had any intention of opening a bookstore," says the affable Paul. "But I got a call from someone offering to sell me some books on Illinois history. I said sure, not realizing he had...five-thousand books."

He took them all, and was in the bookstore business. The current store is the second Prairie Archives location, and it is packed with more than 250,000 books (rare, used, tough-to-find, and new), old campaign posters and buttons, prints, comics, and all manner of intriguing collectibles. There is a Web site (www.prairiearchives.com), and there are T-shirts, the most popular carrying these words: "Abraham Lincoln: They'd have to shoot me to get me back to Springfield."

Though it does attract scholars and collectors, Prairie Archives is a paradise for those who enjoy the quiet pleasures of wandering in the hope of being surprised or of having lively conversations, which Paul or one of the smart members of his staff will gladly provide.

"I sometimes tell people who come in looking for a specific book, 'We have everything but what you want,' " Paul says, with a laugh. "Most people do find something of interest to take home."

The only day it was hard to move around the store was the Saturday in 2007 when, at the Old State Capitol across the street from Prairie Archives, Obama threw his hat into the ring. "Obama's books?" asks Paul. "We did have them, but we're out of stock. We are ordering more."

MARCH 2, 2008

GIVING BACK

You might come upon the Gary Comer Youth Center if you have taken a wrong turn on the way to someplace else, or gone astray while exploring the haunts of our new president's former stomping grounds in Hyde Park/Kenwood to the east. You will not know what to make of it, this strikingly colorful building at 7200 South Ingleside Avenue. It seems of another neighborhood, if not another planet, surrounded as it is by a Grand Crossing area that has been down at the heels for a very long time.

But there it is, the dream made real of Comer, who grew up dirt-poor in Grand Crossing, went on to found clothing retailer Lands' End, made a lot of money, and started giving it back in all manner of ways: buying computers, an air-conditioning system, and uniforms for his old grammar school, Revere; donating more than $80 million to the creation and expansion of the Comer Children's Hospital at the University of Chicago; and building homes for people in the Grand Crossing community. The youth center, a block away from Revere, was built to be the permanent home of the South Shore Drill Team, some of whose three hundred members are performing in Osgood's photo.

And now it is home to Gary Comer College Prep, a campus of the Noble Street Charter School, and every weekday it is filled with the bright, eager faces of the one-hundred-fifty-some members of its first freshman class.

A few years ago Comer, seen in Osgood's photo with a good and famous friend, visited the building when it was still under construction. Though very sick and traveling the hallways in a wheelchair, he still seemed able to see its future.

"Isn't this going to be the greatest thing for the kids?" he said.

He never got to hear an answer, which is a resounding "Yes." He died October 4, 2006.

"Gary always talked about a high school here," said Greg Mooney, executive director of the center. Mooney works closely with Guy Comer, Gary's son and a former commercial airline pilot. Guy's mother, Francie Comer, and his photographer/author sister, Stephanie, are also involved in philanthropic endeavors. But it is Guy who is hands-on here on the South Side, trying to make good on his father's vision.

"People are still poor here. They need help," he said. He shares his father's self-effacing demeanor and his fiery affection for Chicago. He knows that his father has left a lasting legacy. But when you listen to him talk about new ideas and new dreams for this center and this city, you know that in time, that legacy will be his, too.

FEBRUARY 1, 2009

BOSSES

How many aldermen does it take to change a light bulb? I have no idea, so feel free to make up your own joke. The point is that there is a great deal that we do not know about the fifty men and women who, to varying degrees of intelligence, power, and effectiveness, run this city. They are the City Council, the legislative body of Chicago, meeting at least once every month to debate and vote on all manner of things important to the way the city operates. They also oversee, on a more intimate level, the needs, concerns, and complaints of the fifty-five thousand people, on average, who live in their wards.

You might be able to discern a few of the aldermen in Osgood's photo of the City Council chambers but how many of them do you know?

A random survey around the *Chicago Tribune* offices and at various downtown taverns and stores confirmed what we suspected: Not one Chicagoan we asked could name more than a handful of aldermen and a great number of people did not even know the name of the alderman of the ward in which they live.

The reputation of the alderman is understandably shabby, for many have succumbed to the temptation to pocket-stuffing. Many have wound up in prison as a result. The list of such characters and their crimes would gobble up this entire space but the lengthy tradition of corruption in city hall was the reason Mike Royko once suggested that the city's motto be changed from *Urbs in horto*, which means "City in a garden," to *Ube est mea*, which means "Where's mine?"; and why former alderman Dick Simpson titled his wonderful 2001 book about the City Council *Rogues, Rebels, and Rubber Stamps*.

It's not a bad job: $98,000 a year, plus expenses for staff, office, envelopes, and such. For some it's a full-time job; others have separate careers.

In the year 2000, Osgood and I visited every ward, telling you about whatever and whoever caught our eye. Now we visit the wards again, but through the eyes of the aldermen. We asked each one to select something for Osgood to photograph, something in his or her ward that he or she finds particularly significant. It could be a new housing development, a park, business, favorite restaurant, childhood home, place of worship, school, saloon (fat chance), park, person. We are game for anything or anybody.

A November *Chicago Tribune* editorial made a bold suggestion:

"Cut the size of the City Council by half, better yet two-thirds, and let the survivors
tap into the millions of dollars in savings to beef up administrative needs.

With fifty members, Chicago's council is nearly as big as the governing bodies of
Los Angeles, Houston, Detroit, and Philadelphia combined. There's a Chicago ward
for every fifty-five thousand residents. That translates into more bureaucracy, but not
necessarily more efficient or responsive constituent service or more critical analysis
of city issues. The mayor boasts that the city workforce is the lowest it has been
since he took office. But there are fifteen, twenty, twenty-five, even thirty more jobs
he could eliminate, and the city would not be poorer for it."

The year of the aldermen was both fascinating and frustrating,
an extraordinary Sidewalks year. Talking with and getting to know
(fascinating), as best one can in a mere five hundred or so words
(frustrating), the people who have been elected to run the city's
fifty wards has taken us to every corner of Chicago and given us
uncommon insights into how the city works—and doesn't.

This is some of what we heard from . . .

Dorothy Tillman, Third Ward: "Even the aldermen I don't care
for, who are my enemies . . . they all work hard. Sometimes you hear
people say we don't do enough, don't do anything. But then you
will see the smile on the face of a child or someone will thank you for taking care of a problem and
you know that you can make a difference."

Burton Natarus, Forty-second Ward: "I have never bad-mouthed anybody in my campaigns.
Never done that. I don't care what they say about me, and there are a lot of things they could say
about me."

Brian Doherty, Forty-first Ward (the only Republican in the City Council): "The good part of
being the alderman is you're always near home. The bad part is that you're always near home.
Look, I've seen too many guys go to Springfield, ruin their lives, their families. I get paid well in
this job. I like this job."

Ed Burke, Fourteenth Ward: "Wasn't it Lord Acton who said, 'Power corrupts and absolute
power corrupts absolutely?' Do we have to look any further than the scandals in the Catholic

Church? Horrendous. Do we have to look any further than Enron or Arthur Andersen? There is corruption everywhere. Human nature is what it is. We are all prone to make mistakes. I have been fortunate to have the best of both worlds. I have enjoyed the political side of it and also enjoyed my private legal practice. Yes, there have been temptations, [but] if you try to conduct yourself under the rules, in the long run you are better off. But sometimes those rules are changed in the middle of the game. I see some of that in the [criminal charges against former governor George] Ryan case. Frankly I don't see that what George Ryan did was a great deal different than what every other governor has done for the last hundred years."

Interesting as the Sidewalks Aldermanic Year was, none of the characters could match the alderman I first knew.

I never called Mathias Bauler by his familiar nickname, "Paddy," or by the Forty-third Ward title he held from 1933 to 1967, "Mr. Alderman." He was "Grandpa" and "Mr. Bauler." We were just kids, Ty Bauler, Paddy's grandson, and I, best friends growing up a few blocks from the alderman's headquarters in a tavern on the first floor of a brick building. It was in this tavern that Bauler embedded himself in Chicago political history by uttering five words on the night in 1955 that Richard J. Daley was first elected mayor. "Chicago ain't ready for reform," he said.

We knew nothing of that then, or of the night in 1934 when Bauler shot two policemen trying to enter a private party at his tavern; the sensational trial that followed and ended in his acquittal; his having once amused Mayor Anthony Cermak by rolling around on the floor in wrestling matches with his 275-pound self; or his reputation as one of the biggest crooks in City Council history.

We knew nothing about all that, but we knew the alderman had money, and that's what we came for, spending enough time in the tavern for Paddy to ask about school and grades. He bored easily, and so after a couple of minutes he would say, "Here kids, go get some ice cream," and peel bills from a huge roll of money.

Paddy had a lot of money, and he loved to travel. On an impulse, he'd hop a plane and go halfway around the world. One day Paddy who, despite his colorful name, was of German ancestry, decided to go to Munich for a long weekend. He invited my father to go with him.

"Come on, Herm," Paddy said. "We'll have a ball. They got terrific beer gardens in Munich."

My father declined: busy schedule and things like that. But Paddy persisted.

Finally, my father said, "Paddy, I'm Jewish. And Munich is where the Nazi party was born . . . in those very beer halls. So I really don't think I'd feel comfortable being there."

Very slowly, a look of comprehension came over Paddy's fat, round face. Then he put his hand on my father's shoulder and said, "Aw, geez, Herm, why don't you let bygones be bygones?"

WEST SIDE STORY

Y ou may not recognize the face in Osgood's photo, but perhaps you'll remember the name. It is Anne Keegan. For nearly twenty-five years, that was the name (the byline) that sat atop hundreds of *Chicago Tribune* stories.

She was a reporter. She was, as well, a front-page columnist, and for a time, before she was unceremoniously and unfairly forced into an early retirement in 1997, Keegan worked for me. She knew and loved the city and mostly wanted to tell stories about its so-called ordinary people, its outsiders. So she wrote about cops and lawyers, but also about Vietnam veterans and street gangs. She was passionate about writing, and as a result, a Keegan byline above a story meant the delivery of precise reporting and poetic prose.

And now there is a book, a book about a cop named Mike Cronin.

She had talked about this for decades, beginning when she was spending a lot of time with Cronin in the late 1980s. A lot of reporters talk about books—and talk and talk, never finding the time for the more arduous task of sitting down and writing.

Then one day last year, there it was: *On the Street Doing Life: The West Side of Chicago Through the Eyes of a Cop Named 'Cronie.'*

It is a quick and captivating read, with intriguing chapter titles such as "Vietnam, the Double Bubble, and a Mass Card for the Old Man," "I'm a Nut But I'm Me Tonight," "The Girl with the Hole in Her Heart," and "Smash Down the Door... We're Having a Baby."

The book takes the reader into the harsh West Side of the city, where Cronin worked for more than thirty years, much of it in the Gang Crimes Unit.

This is tough territory, a place of few hopes, lots of dope, broken families, and tattered lives but, surprisingly, some real humor. It is a world in which, seemingly, Cronin knows everybody and everybody knows him.

Reading the book, you will get to know the fascinating, if far-too-focused, cop, but you will not ever meet Keegan. Here, as in all her newspaper stories, there is no "I" in her work. She is no wallflower in person, but she seems to lack any self-promotional genes. She didn't do much, hardly anything, to help sell her book. There were no radio or TV appearances, no bookstore signings.

That's just her way, so perhaps it's a good thing she left the newspaper business when she did. In whatever wacky or wonderful ways this business is changing and will continue to change, she just doesn't fit in.

The notion of Keegan having a blog or doing video reports is as unimaginable as Bob Dylan appearing on *American Idol*. She always wanted her work to speak for itself, and it did so, powerfully. Still does.

MAY 4, 2005

HONOR FLIGHT

They were old and weak in body. Many of them were riding in wheelchairs, others used walkers, and a few managed on their own. But as seventy-nine World War II veterans arrived at Midway Airport one Wednesday night in April they were greeted by such an outpouring of emotion and gratitude that you could see the spark of youth in their eyes.

They had had a long day, as part of the latest trip sponsored by Honor Flight Chicago. This not-for-profit organization, with outposts in thirty states, funds and organizes trips for local World War II veterans to Washington, D.C. to visit the World War II Memorial. The first flight took place in the summer of 2008 and they are now scheduled monthly.

More than fifteen hundred people jammed the Midway concourse and the baggage claim area, and it was almost impossible to hear a thing over the shouts and the bag pipes and cheers. Many of these people were the relatives and friends of the veterans, but many others were not: Boy Scout troops, motorcycle clubs, USO volunteers, Chicago cops, military personnel, and others interested in celebrating old soldiers.

Two of them we knew.

Harold Possley, the eighty-seven-year-old father of former *Chicago Tribune* reporter Maurice Possley, was an aviation machinist, third class, stationed in Marshall Islands; he jauntily wore his sixty-six-year-old Navy cap and was with his son Tom, who had accompanied him on the trip. This is what he had to say: "When I was at the memorial, I saw the star with the name of my brother and I was reminded in an overpowering way of how he gave his life for this country. The reception at Midway…I didn't think I was an emotional person, but I had tears in my eyes from the moment I left the plane. The people shaking my hand, the band, the pipers—everyone who was there who made me feel special. It is hard to explain the feeling. That day will live with me until the day I die."

Ellen Miller's father, George J. Miller, was the oldest (ninety-four) and highest ranking (lieutenant colonel) person on the flight, the second oldest to ever make the journey. Though eminently capable of speaking for himself—he is working on his memoirs—we asked his daughter what she thought after accompanying him on the trip. "The day in Washington was cold and rainy, but there were no complaints from the vets. They were the same soldiers they were sixty years earlier: proud and honorable. When we landed at Midway the size of the greeting was a surprise to all of them. The look on my dad's face was unlike any look I have ever seen before. I could see him fighting back the tears. Good soldiers don't cry, but on this special night, even good soldiers cried, and so did everybody else."

MAY 31, 2009

SOUND AFFECTS

Though Osgood and I are (or at least one of us is) too young to remember gathering with family members around a radio and listening to Jack Benny be funny; or to hear the chilling "Who knows what evil lurks in the hearts of men? The Shadow knows;" or *The Lone Ranger*'s stirring, "A fiery horse with the speed of light, a cloud of dust, and a hearty 'Hi-yo, Silver!';" there are many people who not only cling to such memories but are intent on making new ones by bringing the sounds and substance of old radio back to life.

Not all the members of the Those Were the Days Radio Players are old enough to have heard the material they perform at schools, libraries, nursing homes, historical societies, private parties— almost anywhere they are asked to go. Many cast members are relative youngsters, but they all share the belief that the good old radio days were broadcast's most creative, imaginative, and entertaining ones. The Those Were the Days Radio Players were born in December 1991, when Chuck Schaden, acting on an idea proposed by old-time radio fan Tom Tirpak, asked the listeners to his *Those Were the Days* radio program if any of them might like to stage and perform vintage radio shows. The response was stunning. In a week, more than one hundred fifty people had signed up.

There are now eight Those Were the Days Radio Players groups in the area (they do not charge for their shows but instead ask for donations to cover expenses). That's Pauline Messier of the Norridge Those Were the Days Radio Players in Osgood's photo, during a recent performance at the Wilmette Historical Society. This group has fifteen members, including Kay Merkle, who tells us it has performed nearly four hundred shows and notes, "We are people who enjoy entertaining people and bringing radio to life."

Schaden, whose background is in journalism and business, is the only person inducted into the Radio Hall of Fame as a fan. He still broadcasts his program live from 1:00 to 5:00 PM Saturdays on WDCB 90.9 FM, and on the Internet (www.wdcb.org); it's closing in on its fortieth anniversary. (As an example of how wonderfully eclectic this College of DuPage station is, Saturdays begin with acid jazz, a midnight to 5:00 AM gathering of a "form of modern jazz [that] combines hip-hop, soul, and funk elements with the improvisational nature of jazz.").

Schaden still publishes *Nostalgia Digest*, a sixty-four-page quarterly filled—and this is Schaden talking—"with articles about the 'Golden Age' of radio, television, movies, and music, written by those who lived it and those who love it!" The latest edition revealed some fascinating things to me about the late funnyman Danny Kaye.

Over the years we have seen various Those Were the Days Radio Players groups do their thing, and their thing is so enjoyable, it works apart from its historical import. One doesn't need to know the old programs to enjoy them resurrected. These were good shows, good times, and, for some, they evoke great memories.

DECEMBER 16, 2007

THE PROJECTS PROJECT

When you have been a newspaper reporter or a photographer in Chicago for many years, you have had more than a few occasions to enter one of the now-mostly-vanished high-rise buildings that dotted the city and served, for better and worse, as public housing. Osgood and I did so together one day in 1999, and the memory is still with us. We were writing about a teacher at a school in the middle of the two-mile State Street corridor that was the Robert Taylor Homes. Then the largest continuous stretch of public housing in the nation, it contained six of the United States' ten poorest areas with populations of at least twenty-five hundred. The other statistics were equally sad: the Chicago Housing Authority estimated that $45,000 worth of drug

business was done there each day, 95.5 percent of the households were headed by women, 41 percent of adult residents had incomes of less than $5,000 a year, 4 percent were employed.

We were visiting the apartment of one of the seven-year-olds in teacher Karla Kelly's class, and when we asked her why her mattress was on the floor, she said, with chilling matter-of-factness, "Oh, that's for when the people start shooting guns. We won't get killed if we're on the floor."

It is safe to say that many of the memories people have of public housing are not pleasant. But not all was nightmares and hopelessness. For thousands, public housing was salvation. It was home.

The last remaining building of what was the Jane Addams Homes is at 1322 West Taylor Street. It doesn't look like much now. Many hope this building will one day be the home of the National Public Housing Museum. Understandably, this plan strikes some as misguided. As my colleague Blair Kamin recently wrote, there are those who might deem the plan "a gruesome joke—a museum celebrating hellish high-rises?"

The low-rise Addams building, constructed in 1938, was the first federal housing project in Chicago. It has been vacant since 2002, ravaged by the elements. It will take considerable work and money and commitment to transform it, but the nonprofit group spearheading the effort is loaded with important people and ardent supporters, including former CHA residents, U.S. Sen. Dick Durbin, and U.S. Rep. Danny Davis. The mayor likes the idea.

Much money is needed, $17 million. The hope is a 2012 opening.

For generations, politicians and developers have had their way with erasing a lot of the city's past; just have a look at Maxwell Street. But those who lived and worked and slept in public housing should be able to have a place where memories can be evoked. The rest of us need a place to learn.

AUGUST 24, 2008

ANIMAL TALES

Lincoln Park Zoo opens at 7:00 AM. By then, most of its animals have snorted, stretched, wiggled, flapped, and, without benefit of coffee, otherwise roused themselves for another day of exhibiting their easy wonder. Kevin Bell, the zoo's director for more than fifteen years, does have coffee in the morning. One cup. He needs it. He gets to the zoo at 6:00 AM, something he has done almost every day since he was twenty-three and arrived here from New York to become curator of birds, the youngest curator in the zoo's long history.

"I have always known what I wanted to do," Bell says. "I have always known that I would work in zoos. And now, to find myself at the top, with one of the greatest jobs imaginable....But it feels natural to me, and I feel exhilarated."

As much as anyone can be born to a profession—Barry Bonds to baseball, Richard M. Daley to politics—Bell was born to zoos.

He is the son of the late Joseph Bell, the curator of birds and chairman of the department of ornithology at New York's Bronx Zoo. Born in 1952, Kevin was five when he moved with his family into a house on the zoo grounds: "The Boy With 2,830 Pets" shout headlines on faded New York newspapers that Bell keeps in a bulging scrapbook.

He earned a bachelor's degree in biology from Syracuse University and a master's in zoology from the State University of New York. Lincoln Park Zoo director Lester Fisher hired him in 1976.

Lincoln Park Zoo began in 1868, with two pairs of swans donated by New York's Central Park. By 1874 the animal population had swelled to forty-eight birds and twenty-seven mammals. That year a bear was bought for ten dollars and the Lincoln Park Zoological Gardens was officially formed, making our zoo—though arguments come from Philadelphia—the first in the U.S. It has grown—more animals, more land—over the years. It has always been and remains a special slice of the city.

A zoo, especially one as accessible and democratic (free) as Lincoln Park's, sits in a pleasant spot in one's memory and provides a strong thread through one's life. It is a place where virtually every Chicago child is taken by his parents and where, in turn, these children take their children.

Bell says. "People are concerned about the zoo. In a way, they rightly think of it as their own. They feel a warmth toward it," Bell says. "And where else in the world does a boss get to walk around his business and see nothing but people smiling?"

Or, as in Osgood's photo, see a polar bear play a part in a conference on global warming?

Bell's father died in 1986, before Kevin became the father to two young boys, Joseph and Charlie. On some early mornings, they can be seen walking through the zoo together, hand in hand in hand.

DECEMBER 28, 2003

A PIECE OF HOME

You might have seen them, if you were paying attention, amid the crowds wandering the city's busy byways, in groups of three, four, or five, usually, young men and women dressed in the uniforms of the United States armed forces, staring wide-eyed at the city and its sights with what appears to be a mixture of I've-never-been-in-a-big-city-before trepidation and awe.

You would wonder—if you were not too busy understandably worrying about how much weight you were putting on your credit card—what they are doing and how they were feeling far from home during the holidays. Osgood and I saw such a group recently, purposefully making their way to Navy Pier. We said hello, and they told us they were going to the USO, and we realized immediately how little we knew about this organization, beyond what we thought we knew, based on old newsreels of Bob Hope entertaining troops. We decided to learn more.

And so, the USO, which stands for United Service Organizations, was founded in 1941 with the purpose of providing "a home away from home" for those serving in the armed forces. Here in the Chicago area, there are four of these "homes": at the pier, at O'Hare and Midway airports, and at the Great Lakes Naval Station north of Lake Bluff. They offer all manner of help and diversions: Internet access, TVs and video games, free beverages and snacks, referral and information services, housing and transportation, other social services, and emotional support. There are extras: field trips to plays, sporting events, tours of Chicago.

That USO tradition of fine entertainment was continued at an October event in the pier's grand ballroom. "Salute to the Troops" featured Alison Ruble, the USO of Illinois' community and entertainment director, singing in Osgood's photo, and Gary Sinise and his Lt. Dan Band. The emcee was Bill Murray.

"It was a terrific evening, and very moving, too," Ruble said. "I came to this organization seven years ago not knowing much beyond, well, Bob Hope and his shows for troops. I wasn't, frankly, even aware that the USO still existed. I was stunned once I realized everything they were doing, not just to help those in the service, but their families. We probably deal with as many family members as we do those in uniform."

USO of Illinois (www.uso.org/illinois), a not-for-profit, nongovernment-funded organization, serves three hundred thousand military members and their families a year.

It has been hard to remember, in the wake of the joyful hoopla of the presidential election and the crippling fears of the economy, that wars rage across the world, and that some of the young people you see wandering the streets might wind up even farther away, in places far more daunting and dangerous than Chicago at Christmastime.

DECEMBER 21, 2008

LIFE OF PIE

Is it time to pity the pie? That most straightforward of desserts, ancient in origin, has come on hard times. This may have happened years ago, shortly after the invention of flourless chocolate cake. We obviously weren't paying attention until a couple of weeks ago. That's when we were approached by a normal-looking man about sixty years old. It was late afternoon, and we were wandering around the Near North Side.

"Excuse me," the man said. "Do you know where I can get a good piece of pie?"

We said, "Well, there's..." but had no answer.

Though we are not sure there ever was a Golden Age of Pies, they were a big dessert deal for decades. A 1955 menu from the Empire Room in the Palmer House has apple pie listed first among its dessert offerings. The price is fifty cents, a bit less than strawberry parfait, or the intriguing "Frozen Ice Cream Slice." (The same menu offers a sirloin steak for $5.80).

Many fine restaurants still offer sirloin steaks. But pies?

My colleague, restaurant critic Phil Vettel, recently wrote about some of the desserts at Fahrenheit, a new restaurant in St. Charles. "Break out the cameras for the dessert course," he wrote, noting such "picturesque options" as the "PB&J, a collection embracing peanut-butter panna cotta (a smidge oversalted), jelly doughnuts, and a tiny malted milkshake topped with a sliver of crispy potato. The Lemon Meringue is a study in lemon that includes Meyer-lemon curd with some candied lemon rind, a rectangular sugar cookie surrounded by toasted basil meringue, and a ball of lemon-flavored spun sugar resembling cotton candy."

Such "innovations" will probably never make their way to Highland, Wisconsin, a small (population eight hundred fifty-ish) town west of Madison, where you will find Grandma's Kitchen, in business for six years and doing quite well.

Osgood, who functions as the restaurant critic of the Sidewalks team (I tend to handle the taverns), says: "With a name like Grandma's Kitchen, it's got to be good, right? That's what my son Zac and I thought as we drove around looking for some down-home country cooking. We found the atmosphere and food in this eatery to be as genuine as the name, with way too many tantalizing pies to choose from. However, Grandma herself didn't meet our expectations. Instead of a kindly, silver-haired woman in her seventies, she's a charming and experienced cook in her forties."

That woman's name is Tess Bomkamp, and she allowed Osgood to take some photos. I wanted a photo of a piece of pie but Osgood, unknowingly quoting Vettel's article, said that there were too many "picturesque options," and so he took dozens before selecting the photo you see. In addition to pieces of pie, you'll see carrot cake and cherry torte and, after taking his photos, Osgood ate a piece of apple pie. "Delicious," he said.

FEBRUARY 24, 2008

BEING NICE ON ICE

Among the many reasons to hate television is the way it makes most people who skate appear to be demented or depressed. If it's not a sports "highlight" segment giving us one of the boxing matches that liberally punctuate hockey "games," then it's one of those competitions that focus on performers awaiting their scores with the same sort of enthusiasm a person shows while awaiting the results of a biopsy. (And let's just forget the whole Tonya Harding–Nancy Kerrigan fiasco, okay?)

To those who only see skaters on TV, it must seem as if putting on a pair of skates can transform a person into a barroom brawler or a candidate for a psychiatrist's couch.

But those of us who live here are able to see another side of the story, and one chapter was being written on a recent night by those who were gliding, slipping, sliding, and falling all over the ice on the McCormick Tribune Ice Rink in Millennium Park, which was created last winter with $5 million from the Robert R. McCormick Tribune Foundation.

Those entering the new Park Grill restaurant, which fronts the rink, marveled at the number of people outside.

The kids working the rental counter—skating is free, skates are five dollars to rent—were a busy though not talkative bunch.

How many skaters tonight?

"I guess a lot," one girl said.

What do you think is the appeal of skating?

"Huh?" all of them said at once.

Oh, well. Observing a rink, as Osgood was doing at Skate on State, tells you that skating is one of the few sporting activities that can be enjoyed no matter the level of skill. The frustration, anger, and four-letter words one encounters on a golf course or tennis court rarely exist on ice.

Yes, it is different on professional and competitive levels, where stakes are high and fun is just memory. But at any rink around here, when a skater goes down, he or she invariably giggles. When skaters fumble along the railing trying to stay upright, most do so without embarrassment, even with a sort of gleeful determination.

It's almost—almost—enough to make you wish that winter lasted longer.

FEBRUARY 22, 2004

BOOKCLUB, FACE TO FACE

The wild and, so we are told, wonderful world of the Internet remains mostly a mystery to Osgood and me. Of course, we know how to use e-mail and are fond of Google, but we don't do much beyond that. So when we learned that one local Web site, www.gapersblock.com, had its own book club, the unfortunate image that came to mind was of people sitting in their underwear in various apartments and basements around the Chicago area, instant-messaging one another about the latest cyberspace thriller. What a surprise, then, to discover that this book club's members meet, in the flesh (and fully clothed), on the second Monday night of every month at the Book Cellar, that delightful independent bookstore (with wine, beer, coffee, and food) at 4736 North Lincoln Avenue.

The editor and publisher of gapersblock.com is Andrew Huff, thirty-two, who started it with twenty-nine-year-old Naz Hamid in 2003. It is a handsome and well-organized site, a gathering of news, information, and opinion about events, the arts, urban affairs, and other topics, and determinedly and wonderfully Chicago-centric.

It now has, Huff says, four thousand unique visitors each day. But the whole idea is to get people away from their computers.

"That's why we named ourselves gapersblock," says Huff. "We're trying to get people to slow down and check out the city. There's so much going on, in terms of events and projects and the arts, that it's impossible to be bored in Chicago unless you're a hermit."

Upcoming book club titles include *Water for Elephants* by Sara Gruen, *Peel My Love Like an Onion* by Ana Castillo, and *Dreams From My Father* by Barack Obama.

"We'll pick books that are relevant to current events and sometimes classic Chicago reads," says Veronica Bond, the twenty-five-year-old coeditor of the book club. "We've never chosen a book because an author or publisher has asked us to...and they certainly have asked."

Some previous choices have been Elizabeth Berg's *The Year of Pleasure*, a certain book about a Chicago tavern by me, and *Boss: Richard J. Daley of Chicago* by Mike Royko.

The idea for the club came from thirty-two-year-old Alice Maggio, a gapersblock.com editor and librarian. "I started it because I felt people didn't realize what a great literary city Chicago is and has been," she says. "Now the book club is in its third year, and Veronica and I have barely scratched the surface in terms of great books and local authors. Because our focus is local, the people who come to our meetings are not just people who enjoy reading, but who also love this city, and care about Chicago."

JULY 8, 2007

EXTERNAL REST

The poets and deluded baseball managers tell us that the return of warm weather is about rebirth and hope, and so it is with pleasure that Osgood and I give you another cemetery. We do this once in a while to remind you that Chicago's cemeteries are places that combine art, history, and wonder. They are great, not at all ghoulish, attractions. No one has put this better than Ursula Bielski in her book *Graveyards of Chicago*:

> These places are more than mere bone-yards. Though they exist most generically to house tangible remains, they are indeed showplaces of art and architecture, breathtaking expanses of landscape perfection, surprising refuges of nature and silence…

So we've taken you to Graceland, the most famous of the city's burial grounds; to Mt. Emblem Cemetery in Elmhurst, with its ancient windmill; to the mausoleum built for a man named Ira Couch in 1857, and still standing in a part of Lincoln Park that once was Chicago City Cemetery; to Ivanhoe Cemetery, which contains the grave of a man named James Joice, a freed slave who came here after the Civil War; and to Oak Woods Cemetery on the South Side, the final resting place of Enrico Fermi and Ida B. Wells, as well as a "Big Jim" and a "Big Bill" (mobster Giacomo Colosimo and Mayor William Hale Thompson, respectively), and Harold Washington, in a mausoleum with the inscription, REMEMBER ME AS ONE WHO TRIED TO BE FAIR.

And now, on to Rosehill.

Spreading south and east from the intersection of Petersen and Western Avenues—its official address is 5800 North Ravenswood Avenue—Rosehill is the largest cemetery in the city, covering more than three hundred fifty acres. Before it was a cemetery, the area was known as Roe's Hill, named for Hiram Roe, owner of a nearby saloon. A misguided mapmaker, believing he had come across a mistake, "fixed" it. The cemetery accepted its first "customer" in 1859, and now has about two hundred thousand "residents."

Most are not famous, but you will find the tombs of nearly twenty Chicago mayors and many Civil War generals. You will find Oscar Mayer and Aaron Montgomery Ward. There is also the handsome Volunteer Firefighter's Monument, erected in 1864, seven years before the Chicago Fire.

Osgood's photo is of a sculpture at the tomb of Frances M. Pearce and her daughter Frances. They died of illness four months apart, and the husband and father, Horatio Stone, commissioned the statue in their memory. Originally buried in the City Cemetery in Lincoln Park, the bodies later were moved, along with the statue, to Rosehill, where the glass enclosure was added as protection against the elements.

Some say that on the anniversaries of the mother's and daughter's deaths, a mist fills the glass case, and the statues come to life. Yes, ghost stories are also plentiful in local cemeteries.

Talk about rebirth.

JULY 1, 2007

A WRENCHING EXPERIENCE

What the faculty members of Chopper College may lack in Nobel Prizes compared to their "counterparts" at the University of Chicago, they make up for in enthusiasm, tattoos, and catchy nicknames: Clutch, Diesel, and Hammer. They are, respectively, Tommy Creal, Joe Jasko, and Armand Salin.

They are young—twenty-one, twenty-five, and eighteen, respectively—which accounts for the impossible-to-miss sign that hangs from the rafters of the school: "Wisdom is acquired by experience, not just by age." The "campus" is bare bones: a large building with small, attached offices in a drab industrial section of south suburban Harvey. But it is considerably more active than it was four years ago, when Clutch opened a motorcycle-repair business here with "one bench and a stack of tools."

He was pursuing his passions for both bikes and business, which merged at age ten when he began fixing friends' dirt bikes in his parents' garage. He was good at it. After graduating from Mt. Carmel High School, he attended the American Motorcycle Institute in Daytona Beach, Florida.

His repair shop was a success from the start and he was soon doing a lot of custom work. That was the seed of Chopper College. It offers monthly three-day sessions during which groups of five to eight people build a motorcycle from scratch, learning such things as Electrical Basic Components, which entails "…different types of electric systems (main), soldering, shrink wrap, tube crimp connectors…"

"It is intense, ten hours a day," says Clutch. "That's why we call it a 'boot camp.' "

There have been lawyers, bankers, and auto mechanics in the classes; some are serious cyclists, some hobbyists, and others are exploring possible new careers. Wives have bought the classes—the cost is $1,150—as presents for husbands. The students have come from as far away as Europe. Hammer was a student before being hired as an apprentice after his October "graduation."

When classes are not in session, which is most of the time, the "professors" work long and hard repairing and customizing motorcycles. Their shop is a wild gathering of parts and noise and creativity. Some of their finished custom bikes look less like vehicles than works of art.

On one level, a motorcycle is a simple thing, defined by two wheels, a frame, engine and clutch, fork, fuel tank, seat, handlebars, and brakes. As such, it is easy to customize—to "chop"— with parts and materials, paints and designs, that reflect the builder or owner's personal aesthetic.

On another level, of course, there is a macho mystique about the machines—from 6-hp dirt bikes to window-rattling 125-hp Harley-Davidsons—and millions of words have been written trying to explain their appeal and the biker culture, usually evoking such actors and films as Marlon Brando and Lee Marvin in *The Wild One*, Steve McQueen in *The Great Escape*, and Peter Fonda and Dennis Hopper in *Easy Rider*.

Generally, these words wind up being more pretentious and confounding than incisive. Here's what Robert M. Pirsig wrote in his 1974 best seller, *Zen and the Art of Motorcycle Maintenance*:

> A motorcycle functions entirely in accordance with the laws of reason, and a study of the art of motorcycle maintenance is really a miniature study of the art of rationality itself.

Each Chopper College class starts with the students seated at tables. In front of them are massive textbooks covering such topics as "engine, transmission, and primary alignment" and "rake and trail." By the afternoon, they have rolled up their sleeves and started work—questions and answers flying fast—piecing together a chopper from hundreds of parts.

During one class, student Troy Zeidman dropped a screwdriver. "It's amazing that the government allows you to fly helicopters," Jasko said playfully.

"It is, isn't it?" said Zeidman, laughing.

He is a West Point graduate, class of 1998, and a captain in the Army. During his first tour of duty in Iraq, he was a company commander in charge of sixteen Black Hawk helicopters and forty-six soldiers. "The age of the instructors here? That doesn't bother me at all," said Zeidman. "I've got nineteen- and twenty-year-olds working on my helicopters. I trust them with my life and the lives of my men."

Creal, whose past was scarred by troubles with drugs, says, "I feel like I'm the luckiest guy in the world. My parents stood by me. They helped me get this business up and going.... If they didn't have faith in me I wouldn't be here. I would be dead or lost.... Make that dead. But I now can see the future and it looks good. I'm thinking we might have to add another floor, a second floor with classrooms. I can see us opening campuses in Florida and Seattle. I can, in a few years, see a lot of Chopper Colleges."

The motto of the University of Chicago is *Crescat scientia; vita excolatur*, which is Latin for "Let knowledge grow from more to more; and so be human life enriched."

Chopper College has yet to adopt a motto, but until a better one comes along, I'll settle for this: "Wisdom is acquired by experience, not just by age."

SENIOR SEMINARS

What you see when you walk toward the North Shore Senior Center on any day is a parking lot filled with cars. "You think they are giving away free Fountain of Youth pills?" Osgood asks, hopefully. The building, housed in what was a massive warehouse for a scuba-diving company in Northfield, is a beautifully renovated structure, painted mostly white and filled with light and activities. There are dozens every week, most of them free, from computer classes to a discussion of *The Iliad*. There are meetings of the bridge club, Yiddish club, and photography club. Every Tuesday, the Men's Club has lectures on topics as varied as "Civil Liberties in the Age of Terrorism" and "Traveling in Vietnam and Cambodia."

There are any number of field trips to places such as the Indiana Dunes. There are a lot of health and fitness programs, most held in a handsome fitness center, and many about the arts. The folks in Osgood's photo, Carol Salinger, seventy-six, and Stanley Cohen, eighty-three, are participating in a painting class.

"It's like college without any grades," Osgood says.

Some of the numbers are striking: forty-two hundred people enrolled in lifelong learning classes, more than seven hundred volunteers for thirty-five activities, nearly forty thousand people in twenty-three communities participating in programs.

One of the volunteers is Joan Golder, a delightful woman and a past president of the center's board. She is here every Tuesday to do whatever needs to be done. "It is a wonderful thing to watch people as they reinvigorate their lives. We don't have bingo here," she says. "There is a stigma attached to that when it comes to seniors. There are still a lot of stigmas. So we don't have bingo. Instead we have so much else, so many ways for people to keep growing and learning. Being here, seeing that, is just thrilling to me."

But what you see is not all you get, for behind the classes and lectures and programs is a vast area of offices where people are dealing with the many social services essential to the elderly and their families.

The majority of the fifty-two-year-old, not-for-profit center's annual budget of nearly $7 million goes to counseling, assistance, and information for such social services as elder-abuse intervention, money management, adult day care, escorted transportation, tax preparation, and dozens more, including, inevitably, end-of-life planning.

"These services provide guidance," Golder says, "but they also give independence."

Osgood and I have visited a lot of senior centers over the years to talk about our work. Of course, some of these places are better than others—better funded, larger, prettier, more crowded. But they are all, North Shore Senior Center in particularly vibrant fashion, filled with life.

JUNE 22, 2008

ALL YOU NEED IS CAKE

The crowd was three hundred strong and filled with smiling faces of all, or almost all, ages. It jammed the sidewalk near the Hard Rock Hotel and was in a celebratory mood, which was a good thing, because they were gathered to celebrate the sixty-eighth birthday of Ringo Starr on July 7. And so they sang "Happy Birthday" and flashed peace signs and made Ringo so happy that he said, as TV cameras focused on his smiling face, "What a great birthday gift. If you could pan around, you could see Chicago is full of peace and lovers."

Following tradition, there was a birthday cake; following public-relations protocol, the sheet cake bore the Hard Rock logo. There were also small cupcakes, which Ringo distributed and the crowd ravenously devoured. Many would have been surprised to learn that they had not come from one of the fine and chic bakeries that dot the city's tonier neighborhoods, but rather from an oasis on the South Side, the Perfect Peace Cafe & Bakery, 1255 West Seventy-ninth Street, in the Auburn Gresham neighborhood.

It is a most pleasant place, which began when Denise Nicholes met her future business partner, Julie Welborn, through the youth ministry at Saint Sabina, the nearby church.

They shared a dream of owning a restaurant and formulated a business plan more than five years ago. They dreamt, they planned, they found a space, and—with assistance and guidance from Saint Sabina's Rev. Michael Pfleger, neighborhood businesses, and students with the legal clinic of the University of Chicago Law School—they opened in July 2007.

The menu is ambitious, with many sweets and treats, some based on family recipes, but also with a sophisticated offering of salads, sandwiches (among them a grilled chicken panini with pesto sauce and red peppers), and soups (among these, chicken tortilla).

"A lot of people tell us this is the sort of place they would expect to find in Hyde Park or Beverly," Nicholes says. "Or even on the North Side."

It is difficult to start a business, any business, especially in these precarious economic times, and especially in neighborhoods that feature as many boarded-up stores as those that are open. Though the cafe has received some media attention, surprisingly there has, so far, been no cash register bump from the Ringo Starr event.

"No, really, nothing yet," Nicholes says. "A few people who come in have heard about us through TV, but mostly it's word of mouth, and most of the comments are thanking us for opening in this neighborhood."

Hey, you three hundred people who liked the free cake and cupcakes at Ringo's birthday party, it's not such a long and winding road from Michigan Avenue down to Seventy-ninth Street. Make the trip.

AUGUST 31, 2008

A RIVER RUMBLES THROUGH IT

On some days, especially in winter, Chicago seems most enjoyable to us in the shadows and rumbles that exist beneath the "L." This is not what boosters and civic leaders tout—*How much prettier you'll find the Bean! Get over to Navy Pier!*—but whenever we walk those streets that sit under the "L" tracks, the city feels alive and mysterious and gritty and real. This experience is, of course, most accessible downtown, beneath the tracks that form what is commonly referred to as the Loop: Wabash Avenue on the east, Wells Street on the west, Lake Street on the north and Van Buren Street on the south. Bathed in a hard shade even on the sunniest days, this is a walk guaranteed to remind you that you live in a place of sometimes-hidden and often-harsh beauty.

Another stretch extends for about a mile above Sixty-third Street, between Cottage Grove Avenue and Martin Luther King Jr. Drive.

Part of the CTA's Green Line, this section of track is among the city's oldest. It once extended east to Jackson Park, where it unloaded passengers giddily rushing to enjoy the diversions and marvels of the Columbian Exposition of 1893. After the fair closed, the line was amputated to Stony Island Avenue, and in more recent years it lost additional track and stops at Dorchester and University Avenues.

We can remember how rough and tumble and terrifying that bygone eastern stretch was, filled with some thirty bars and liquor stores. Known as "Baby Skid Row," it was freed from the overhead tracks in 1997, and in short order the street-level seediness and crime began to vanish. You will now find that strip dotted with new homes carrying high price tags.

But where the "L" still stands, the walk under it takes you past a couple of liquor stores and bars, some retail stores, the handsome Bessie Coleman Branch of the Chicago Public Library (which opened in 1992), other new buildings, and a large number of empty lots.

It will introduce you to Daley's Restaurant, which boasts surprising longevity—"since 1918"—even though it is actually older, opened in 1892 by a man who was no relation to the local political clan. Until the 1960s, it was a fine-dining, steak-and-wine kind of place. Then, reflecting the changing demographics of the Woodlawn neighborhood, it became and remains a tasty and friendly soul-food stop.

The "L" rumbles above. People eat and talk. Osgood shoots.

There is a certain airy poetry (and a lot of sky) in Osgood's photo. And there is the urge, always, when writing of the "L," to evoke that poet Nelson Algren, and so I will: He called it "the city's rusty heart." We told this to a man we met standing at the corner of Sixty-third and Cottage Grove, in the shadow of tracks and station. He looked up and said, after a long moment, "Hmmm. I like to think of it more like a river."

JANUARY 28, 2007

BOOKS ARE COOKING

Lois Weisberg, the city's commissioner of cultural affairs, seems to get an idea as often as the rest of us take a breath. Some never leave her third-floor office in the Chicago Cultural Center, the magnificent building on Michigan Avenue between Randolph and Washington Streets. But many do, percolating in the minds of her staff (who actually become something closer to collaborators) and finally manifesting in some event that enlivens the city for a time, annually or perhaps for keeps.

So, one day a year or so ago, into Weisberg's office walks Danielle Chapman, a young poet. The two women talk, they discuss books and writers, then part. Chapman is excited, and things start to happen. "Lois wanted to do for the local publishing industry what she has been able to do for our arts, culinary, and fashion scenes," Chapman says.

And so, there in Osgood's photo, you see the first and most accessible expression of this idea-made-real: a new literary gallery flanking the grand staircase on the Cultural Center's north side. That's Weisberg (right) and Chapman, who now has the title director of literary arts and events.

"Who would know we had so many publishers?" Weisberg asked on the night of the gallery's opening in October. The works of more than seventy local book publishers and one hundred twenty periodical publishers were represented in more than fifteen hundred books, magazines, journals, zines, comics, and other paper items.

That night there was a panel conversation (moderated by me) that featured Dominique Raccah, founder of the largest woman-owned publishing company in the United States, Sourcebooks; Haki Madhubuti, poet and publisher of the largest African-American-run publishing company in the country, Third World Press; artist and author Audrey Niffenegger; and Jonathan Messinger, books editor for *Time Out Chicago*, author, and copublisher of featherproof books.

There was a party afterward, and all of those attending were, in the words of Susan Betz, "stunned." "I'm getting to see some old faces, but was amazed and so encouraged that there are so many new faces," said Betz, a senior editor at Chicago Review Press.

Equally impressed was Sharon Woodhouse, founder and owner of Lake Claremont Press. "Consider the potential here...the talent, passion, and diversity of companies in the room," she said.

And that's the whole idea. Chapman is planning events and gatherings for the future, fully aware that no matter how many books line shelves (according to Bowker, which tracks the industry, some 275,000 titles and editions are published each year in the United States), publishing is a tough business. But she and Weisberg are pleased so far, especially seeing people again reading books in the building that was for decades the main branch of the Chicago Public Library, sort of a publishers' heaven.

JANUARY 11, 2009

A CLEAN, WELL-LIGHTED PLACE

Writers write. That may seem obvious, and it is, but where and how writers write is fascinating. Ernest Hemingway is said to have written standing up, five hundred to a thousand words a day. William Faulkner supposedly sipped whiskey while at his desk. Chicago's Scott Turow wrote while riding the train from his home in the north suburbs to his law offices downtown. I didn't check on the habits of the writers hanging out at the Writers WorkSpace, 5443 North Broadway. It's never a good idea to interrupt a writer at work, and that is what, to varying degrees of enjoyment and success, one has to imagine they were doing. The place's purpose is "to provide a comfortable and inspiring shared studio where writers can concentrate on their personal and professional work and enjoy as much or as little community as they want."

It's a lovely idea. Though I am not so inclined, I know many writers who need to talk about agents, moan about publishers, and whine about sales with other writers; to share ideas with other writers, or steal ideas.

This is the place for them. The cost of membership, $125 a month, may seem a bit much for a starving poet's pocketbook, but you get free fax and copier machines, Wi-Fi and printers, meeting rooms, a kitchen, and beverages (not booze). And who can put a price on "community"?

It is a pleasant space, and certainly beats the hustle and bustle of a coffee shop. And just think of the creative buzz with all those novels abuilding.

The man in Osgood's photo is not a writer. He is Lowell Thompson, a painter whose work adorns the walls. He began painting after a long career in advertising, and his work is compelling. It focuses on the city "they don't show in glossy guides for tourists."

Nelson Algren would feel a kinship, and might also appreciate Thompson's way with words: "There are only two kinds of people in Chicago. Those that get the blues and those that give 'em."

Some writer might easily build a short story, novel, or oeuvre around that observation. Though I hope to soon pick up a book and see the WorkSpace in the acknowledgments, I am of that era when writers found comfort and inspiration in taverns. But I also heard too many great ideas tossed (and lost) into the air rather than put down on paper.

One night many years ago, a local author was squiring a famous, best-selling author from New York around town. They stopped in O'Rourke's, then a favorite hangout for the literary set on North Avenue. It was a typically boisterous Friday night, and the local author proudly stretched his arms out at the chattering crowd.

"This is what Chicago writers do," he said.

The famous author pondered this for a moment.

"Writers write," he said. And then he walked out the door.

JULY 6, 2008

ODE TO TERRY

Death is no way to end a year, and dying at forty-six is no way to end a life. Terry Armour was forty-six when he died December 29, 2007. Maybe you read about it in the papers, or heard about it on radio or TV. Armour, who wrote for the *Chicago Tribune*, had been a star in all mediums. The death was sudden, due to a pulmonary embolism. The shock was hard and intense, and, a few days later, the funeral was a shower of tears.

Perhaps you haven't thought about him in a while. That's okay, understandable. Things move on.

Armour's desk and cubicle in Tribune Tower sit vacant, awaiting another reporter, perhaps, or just more emptiness. Sometimes, someone around here will say, "Hey, remember when Terry...," but it happens less and less often.

There is one person, however, who thinks about Armour all the time.

"If you have a choice, be the one to go first," says LaNell Armour, who was Terry's wife. "Being a survivor sucks."

She is sitting in Stefani's 437, a restaurant on the corner of Rush and Hubbard Streets. This was where Terry took her on their first date.

"We sat at that table near the door, and he was so proudly introducing me to everyone who came in," she says. "He was....He is unforgettable."

She has yet to return to her profession and to the sixy-some kids she had been teaching to play the piano. She keeps busy planning a memorial, set to take place September 22 at U.S. Cellular Field, which was, for Terry, a kind of heaven on earth. That date would have been his forty-seventh birthday.

"I want anybody who wants to come to come. The whole city can come," says LaNell.

There is comfort, too, in the dog, Kramer, that she and Terry took home from the Anti-Cruelty Society late last year. And there is comfort in her Downstate parents and Terry's in-town family, especially his mother, Elaine. They talk at least once every day.

Stefani's 437 was once called Riccardo's, and it was a hangout for, among others, many of the reporters and editors who worked at the four nearby newspapers. The more famous of these are memorialized by photos on the restaurant's walls.

"Terry was a great guy," says the restaurant's owner, Phil Stefani. "He lit up a room."

A few days after LaNell visited the restaurant, Stefani and manager Frank Giannelli put a framed photo of Terry on the wall: Big smile and immortality, of sorts.

You can see it, next to Carl Sandburg.

JUNE 8, 2008

OAK PARK SISTERHOOD

Oak Park, looking hipper every time we drive through or stop to visit friends, is still home to ghosts. The most prominent, of course, is that of architect Frank Lloyd Wright. It was his ghost, and that of his lover, Mamah Borthwick Cheney, that so haunted Oak Parker Nancy Horan she was compelled to put their life together in the form of a novel. The critically praised, best-selling *Loving Frank* is now conveniently out in paperback for the proverbial beach read.

You can easily get a Wright fix there, or via the many tours that showcase his work in the suburb. Osgood and I have read the book and taken the tours, and so decided to explore one of Oak Park's lesser-known landmarks, a place that in many ways lives up to its name, the Nineteenth Century Club.

It was founded by a group of women in 1891, when many women were not allowed to partake of the intellectual party and were cut out from civic involvement. One of those founders was Anna Lloyd Wright, mother of, well, guess who. You just can't escape him out here.

For more than a century, the club and its members, some of whom you can see in Osgood's photo at one of the twice-monthly gatherings of its bridge club, have enriched their community and their own lives.

It has changed with the times. Its most recent mission statement, from 1997, says the club "promotes social responsibility and life-long learning by providing philanthropic opportunities and multicultural programs for an intergenerational, ethnically diverse audience."

Lofty goals, and good ones. And we hope that the club continues to follow through. It gets harder every year, though, because of a lack of new blood. There are ongoing efforts to attract younger members, but that is difficult with all of the cocktail-networking options available to the just-out-of-college crowd.

Some youngsters might giggle at the notion of playing bridge, or be too embarrassed to admit to belonging to an institution that proudly touts its sewing club. Keep sneering, if you can, when I tell you that these items, made by the ladies in that club, are given to those in need.

The club is housed in a two-story Classical Revival building with gracious indoor spaces and a ballroom. It has been the club's home since 1928 and was designed by James L. Fyfe.

The building is often rented for weddings and other affairs, and it all but echoes with the sounds and voices of its past, especially the weekly programs that have featured all sorts of interesting types.

Osgood and I somehow were allowed to join a distinguished roster of speakers that includes Amelia Earhart, Carl Sandburg, Bertrand Russell, and Jane Addams. And walking out of the club, we could almost hear the ghosts of those folks in lively, ongoing conversation.

AUGUST 3, 2008

LIVE, FROM CHICAGO, IT'S . . .

It would be impossible—we know, we actually tried—to calculate the number of live performances Osgood and I have seen in our decades on this planet. There have been many thousands, to be sure. A lot came just for fun, or as part of our duties for various newspapers, and many are with us still: Billy Petersen playing killer Jack Henry Abbott at Wisdom Bridge; the final performance together by Frank Sinatra, Dean Martin, and Sammy Davis Jr. at the Chicago Theater; the Who at the Kinetic Playground; Jim Morrison and the Doors at the Auditorium . . .

The list is, as I said, long.

"I'll never forget . . . ," Osgood would begin a sentence, and then colorfully recall shows by Bonnie Koloc, one of our favorites from many nights, and dozens of others. Of the performers and performances that have faded from our minds, some deserve that darkness. Others are gone just as part of the aging process, as craftily captured by poet Billy Collins (we saw him give a reading at the Chicago History Museum a few years ago) in the end of his poem "Forgetfulness":

> Whatever it is you are struggling to remember,
> it is not poised on the tip of your tongue,
> not even lurking in some obscure corner of your spleen.
> It has floated away down a dark mythological river
> whose name begins with an L as far as you can recall,
> well on your own way to oblivion where you will join those
> who have even forgotten how to swim and how to ride a bicycle.
> No wonder you rise in the middle of the night
> to look up the date of a famous battle in a book on war.
> No wonder the moon in the window seems to have drifted
> out of a love poem that you used to know by heart.

The man in Osgood's photo is A. J. Martin, who performs as the one-man rock band Slow Gun Shogun. Martin was playing at the Empty Bottle, 1035 North Western Avenue, a club, like many here, that has admirably been in the business, in addition to presenting established and well-known acts, of nurturing new talent.

I know we are all, or should be, trying to trim back on expenses. But there is nothing frivolous and everything enriching about paying to see live performances, and listings for such in the *Chicago Tribune* and other publications are a feast of the affordable and free. You just have to think outside your I-only-like-such-and-such box. You never know. You might find something that stays with you for keeps.

JANUARY 25, 2009

ARNIE'S BIG PARTY

Very, very few of the hundreds of thousands of you who have been stuffing your faces for the last nine days, and will continue to do so through Monday, at Taste of Chicago, ever had the pleasure of knowing the man who knew how hungry you really were. He was Arnie Morton, and he died May 28 at eighty-three. He invented Taste.

He grew up in a South Side restaurant family and ran the food and beverage operations for the Playboy clubs and resorts. He almost single-handedly reinvigorated the Rush Street nightlife area when he opened Arnie's at 1050 North State Street in 1974.

With its gloriously garish Richard Himmel design, fine food, and upscale customers, Arnie's profoundly influenced the local dining scene.

The first Taste of Chicago was held July 4, 1980, on Michigan Avenue between Ohio Street and Wacker Drive. It was a smash. Two hours after the 10:00 AM opening, the wait to buy tickets

needed to sample food from forty restaurants was thirty minutes (prices for food items ranged from fifty cents to $2.50). A frazzled but excited Morton told a reporter, "Right now, I'd say things were a little out of control.... I'll do this again under any circumstances."

And he did, again and again and again. (Osgood's photos are from the 1991 Taste).

Some of his other ideas (a Grand Prix race in Chicago) were pleasantly nutty and never realized. Some—Zorine's, a private disco named for his wife, and Arnie's North and Brio restaurants—lived and died.

One of his ideas turned into a tremendous success: Morton's, the steakhouse he opened in 1978, grew into an empire. Arnie sold his interest but watched with pride as more than sixty Morton's restaurants opened across the country.

He was a good and decent man, his quiet manner and humility in surprising but charming contrast to the flash of his restaurants.

And so, perhaps before this year's Taste is done, you might want to put down that turkey leg long enough to thank Morton for all the fun and calories you've had.

JULY 3, 2005

TICKET TO READ

Sitting behind the counter at Read Between the Lynes, a bookstore on the town square in Woodstock, is a massive and lethargic six-year-old St. Bernard named Mia. "She's not herself. We got a new puppy," says Arlene Lynes, who owns the store and Mia. "She'll perk up." Lynes is confident because it is Wednesday morning and the store, as cozy and well-stocked as any member of that besieged breed known as the independent bookstore, is filling with the bright eyes and high-pitched giggles of little kids. It's the same every Wednesday and Saturday morning, when the store hosts Storytime, just one in an ever-growing number of regular activities, special events, and author visits. "These are things that make for a community," says Lynes, whose three children are too old for Storytime.

The person reading today is Debora Mitts-Smith. She has a PhD in children's literature and teaches at Dominican University. More intriguingly, she and her husband and kids live in what is commonly referred to around here as the *Groundhog Day* house. It "played" the Cherry Street Inn in the 1993 movie, and was where the weathercaster, played by Bill Murray, was awakened at 6:00 AM morning after morning after morning by a radio blaring Sonny & Cher's "I Got You Babe."

As the children and their mothers (not a dad in sight) begin to gather around Mitts-Smith at the back of the store, the woman behind the counter beams. "It's been so nice to watch the kids grow and change," says Leslie Schubert, who has been a knowledgeable employee since the store opened two years ago.

The youngest children sit on mothers' laps, and a few nuzzle up to Mia, whose presence compels Mitts-Smith (far right in Osgood's photo, with Lynes behind her) to begin by reading *Harry the Dirty Dog*. The following thirty minutes make for a charming scene, all these little brains paying attention to spoken words, getting an early—and one can hope lasting—taste of books' beguiling powers.

Woodstock had been without a bookstore for five years when Lynes opened hers in 2005. She had done her homework, eventually traveling with her husband, Keith, who is in the computer business, to Florida to take a five-day course titled, simply enough, "How to Open an Independent Bookstore." But there is nothing simple about trying to do battle with the book-retailing giants.

"My philosophy is to offer personal service," says Lynes. "We have come to know so many of our customers—hate to even use that word, 'customer.' These are friends."

The morning's Storytime ends with a stirring reading of *Pinocchio*, though many of the kids appear to have more fun with the book that was read before, *If My Dad Were a Dog*. By that time, though we can't be sure, Mia seemed to have forgotten her troubles.

SEPTEMBER 9, 2007

THE SIGNS OF A TIME

Osgood and I love signs, especially signs of places that no longer exist, signs such as the one atop the Allerton Crowne Plaza Hotel just east of Michigan Avenue. The Tip Top Tap was the building's twenty-third-floor bar that closed in the 1960s. Most signs of bygone businesses are not so prominent. Most exist as painted names or pictures on brick walls. You barely notice.

I bring this up because I recently came across an old paperback, *The Chicago GuideBook*, put together by the editors of the *Chicago Guide*, which was the predecessor of what is now *Chicago* magazine. It was published in 1972 and the cover price was $1.95, not bad at all when you consider the amount of information crammed into its 240 pages.

What it does is take us on a fascinating trip back to a city that no longer exists. Yes, the grand cultural institutions listed in the book are still here, the zoo, the planetarium. But what of the city's less-prominent features and diversions? Gone are the restaurants L'Escargot, The Flying Frenchman, Alexander's, That Steak Joynt, Armando's, and dozens more.

Just looking at the listing for The Embers on Walton Street—"intimate and comfortable"—brought back to memory an evening once spent there in the company of the great writer Irwin Shaw. How many of you might get a similarly delightful and, frankly, boozy flashback, seeing the listings for such bygone nightclubs as Orphans, Quiet Knight, or Mr. Kelly's, or even the Blue Max?

By rough calculation, more than half of the places in the book no longer exist. Some are more painful to recall than others: the cozy Oak Street Bookstore, that dark, subterranean billiard parlor called Bensinger's. Great, great places.

Don't get us wrong. Osgood and I know that the city is meant to change. It has to change. It is, in a very real sense, a living thing. It must keep moving.

But why do we so easily forget?

Perhaps it is because there are not enough visual reminders of the city's past. There is, bless it, the Tip Top Tap. But sometimes it feels like all we have are the yellowing pages in an old book, or some words and pictures on brick walls, growing fainter as each season passes.

NOVEMBER 25, 2001

CHICAGO'S STORYTELLER

hen I was hired by the *Chicago Tribune* in the late summer of 1989, one of my first tasks was to update the obituary of Studs Terkel. It has long been a common practice at many newspapers, at least those with an extra body to spare, to create obituaries of notable people at about the time those people begin to go gray. There has never been a hard and fast rule about the making of these "standing obits," but there are more than a few celebrated citizens who would be surprised to learn that their deaths have already been anticipated in *Tribune* prose. Studs—it just doesn't seem right, even though it is editing policy, to refer to him as Terkel; his real first name, by the way, is Louis—was a vibrant seventy-seven years old, and the obituary had been originally drafted by an anonymous writer (or writers) in 1983. I did my bit, adding the accomplishments during those six years, massaging some awkward sentences, and leaving blank the spaces to be later filled with the details of death—time and place and cause— and for quotations from notable people attesting to Studs' stature and significance.

Occasionally, when a health crisis occurred (and there were a few serious ones), I would further update the obituary. Then it would sit, gathering computer dust, as Studs kept moving.

Studs is ninety-five now, and the shadow is closing in. He has withered. To touch his arms through the red-checkered shirt that has been part of his familiar sartorial ensemble for many decades (along with red socks, dark pants, and blue blazer), is to feel a living skeleton. To sit with him, even as he displays a mind still sharp with its ability to recall names and dates and places from his lengthy and storied past, is to know that his final day is coming. He knows this, too.

"Remember those old Ivory soap commercials, 'Ivory Soap, 99.44 percent pure?' Well I am 99.44 percent dead," he is saying, sitting in the sun-soaked living room of his North Side house. The place is a mess, though not as disordered as in years past, when he was juggling his careers and passions and his wife, Ida, was doing her best to keep up with the hurricane of papers, tapes, books, letters, photos, and visitors that so pleasantly cluttered their life.

Ida died on the night before Christmas Eve in 1999. She and Studs had been married for more than sixty years, and many felt that, given how much Studs relied on Ida for, well, almost everything, Studs was a goner.

"It's hard. It's very hard," he said the day she died. "She was seven days older than me, and I would always joke that I married an older woman. That's the thing: Who's gonna laugh at my jokes? At those jokes I've told a million times? That's the thing....Who's gonna be there to laugh?"

Without the laughter, there was work. Since Ida's death, Studs produced more books; appeared and spoke at dozens of rallies for various causes and literary events; sat for interviews with hundreds of reporters and TV types.

Now, there is one more.

It is his memoir, *Touch and Go*, the title taken from a poem by Dylan Thomas.

> And every evening at sun-down
> I ask a blessing on the town
> For whether we last the night or no
> I'm sure it's always touch and go."

Thomas is most famous for another poem that begins,

> Do not go gentle into that good night,
> Old age should burn and rave at close of day;
> Rage, rage against the dying of the light.

There is still rage in Studs, and it is usually directed at those long-standing targets of social injustice: numbskull politicians, poverty, and war. A gentle autumn breeze blows through the window, ruffling the pages of the book on his lap.

"My book, I've wanted to write it for a long time," he said. That time finally came in 2004. On July 4, Studs took a terrible fall in his home. He was rushed to the hospital, where he underwent surgery to repair a fractured neck. He spent months recovering.

After the operation, publisher Andre Schiffrin suggested to Studs' longtime collaborator, author Sydney Lewis, that she fly to Chicago from her home in Massachusetts and start working with Studs on a memoir. "He told me: If it works, great; if not, it's a good way to keep Studs company," says Lewis. "It was, on many levels, a labor of love."

Lewis worked for many years at WFMT, Studs' radio home for nearly half a century, but the two met before that. "I was a waitress at the [Belmont Avenue music club] Quiet Knight and Studs was there for a benefit for the Wobblies [Industrial Workers of the World]," she says. "I was waiting on his table and all he did was ask me questions, 'Where are you from? 'What do you think about...?' After a while I just had to tell him, 'Look, Studs, I loved *Working* but I *am* working.' "

That lovely anecdote is not in *Touch and Go*. At 253 pages, there is only so much that can be packed in. Do the math: that's about 2.7 years a page. By comparison, the slender new biography of twenty-six-year-old Cubs pitcher Carlos Zambrano has more than six pages per year.

The book is dedicated to Studs' only child, Dan, about whom he writes: "Learning from those I interviewed that I needed them helped me when the time came, when Ida died, when I needed my son and in many ways we needed each other."

JR Millares has been Studs' caregiver since 2004. "[He] was more than a caregiver," Studs writes in his new book. "He was hip to all the nuances; his help immeasurable."

Studs is never alone. Millares works eighty-four hours a week, with his son, Paul, and Dan Terkel taking the rest. "It has been very interesting and rewarding," says Millares, who came to the U.S. from his native Phillipines in 1996. "He is the only person I have ever cared for who has no mental disabilities. He's as sharp as a razor."

"I admire his interest in life. After him I don't know if I would be able to care for anyone else. This has been so lively, so filled with activity. I think I may have to start a new career."

"Studs has that thing that all kids have, that delight, wonder, and joy in things," Lewis says. "Everything is exciting. Everything can be connected. It's that jazz of waking up every day that keeps him going."

Well, one day he will not wake up. In August 2005, Studs had a successful open-heart procedure to replace a narrowed aortic valve and redo one of five coronary bypasses he underwent nine years earlier.

A few days later he asked his doctor, "How long do you give me?"

"I'll give you to ninety-nine," said the doctor.

"That's too long," said Studs. "I think I want a nice round figure, like ninety-five."

And so, here he is, ninety-five years old, and telling me, with zest, that he wants to be cremated and have his ashes mixed with those of his wife, which sit in an urn in the living room of his house, near the bed in which he sleeps and dreams. He wants them to be scattered in Bughouse Square, the patch of park across from Newberry Library where he spent many of his formative years, wide-eyed at the words pouring from the assortment of lunatics, philosophers, intellectuals, and radicals who got up on soapboxes to speak.

"Scatter us there," he says, a gleeful grin on his face. "It's against the law. Let 'em sue us."

On May 17, 2009, that's what a small bunch of us did, scattered those ashes under a newly planted tree. I had known Studs my entire life. He came to the hospital the night of my birth to take my father out for a celebratory drink. They should both know this: So far, no lawsuits.

SCULPTOR OF SOUNDS

Ian Schneller is a luthier, he will proudly tell you. He could just as easily call himself a musician or a sculptor, for he has been, and remains, both. But "luthier" (one who makes stringed instruments) seems to suit him best at the moment. It is an old word, and Schneller is thinking about old guitars, guitars made during the Renaissance that feature inlays of hunting scenes. But he is also thinking about the future, the six Renaissance-style guitars he will soon begin to make, and wondering: "Where will they be in one hundred years? Will they be preserved? Still played?"

There are all sorts of creative people, but few of them have been able to merge two creative impulses into a successful and satisfying career. Schneller's company, Specimen Products, currently moving from its Division Street location to new digs on Homan Avenue, is revered by those in the music business. It repairs, restores, and services guitars and tube amplifiers, and has a large stock of vintage and used guitars and other instruments, as well as cords, strings, and other musical necessities. But what makes it a musical mecca are the custom instruments Schneller builds.

When he came to Chicago from Memphis to attend graduate school at the School of the Art Institute, he was a sculptor of playful constructions that included toys. He also played music. A member of the band Shrimp Boat (and later Falstaff), he began making instruments in 1987, first for himself and later for friends, and discovered that for "the first time there was a need, a desire, for what I was making."

Schneller's creations take a long time to make. In fifteen years, he estimates, he has handcrafted only a few more than one hundred.

"It has been a learning process," he says. "It was humbling, and I had to discipline myself to learn. The service end of the business has been critical to my development as a luthier."

In Osgood's photo, Schneller is holding the model for what will be a larger tube amp, based on the shape of old phonograph horns. He has a number of commissions he must finish before beginning "physical work" on his Renaissance guitars. He wants to perform on stages again, to play. And he is eager to see the band Low perform, because its member Alan Sparhawk plays an aluminum guitar Schneller made.

When he does get that opportunity, he will feel, he says, "like a nervous parent." But he will also feel a warmth. Long ago, when he would show his sculpture in galleries, he felt that there was something "icy, static to it." When he sees and hears one of his instruments played, he feels they are "active parts of our society."

MARCH 24, 2002

PEARL OF OLD TOWN

Gail Leslie, a real estate agent who lives in California, walked into Twin Anchors recently, turned to the right and, with expressions of shock and disappointment, said loudly, "The bowling game! Where's the shuffle bowling game?"

"Well," said a bourbon-drinking man leaning on the bar. "They took that out, oh, twenty years ago."

"That's not fair," said Leslie. "I was just in Butch McGuire's and asked for Butch, and the bartender started to cry and told me Butch died last year."

Of course, it was unreasonable for her to expect things not to change, especially since she has spent the last twenty-five years far from her old local haunts.

The disappearance of a bowling game (they could no longer find parts to repair it) cannot diminish the appeal of this venerable place. Yes, the crowd looks younger than one might remember. Yes, there are a few more healthy items on the menu, in addition to the renowned baby back ribs. And there are many more celebrated faces in frames on the walls.

But Twin Anchors remains a comforting landmark in a city that often seems intent on erasing parts of its past for the sake of trendy pleasures and the benefit of checkbook-wielding developers.

It started its life in 1910 as a tavern on the southeast corner of Sedgwick and Eugenie Streets in the heart of Old Town, and then, during those misbegotten days of enforced—sort of—national abstinence, it was a speakeasy.

Bob Walters and Herb Eldean, both members of the Chicago Yacht Club (Eldean was the Monroe Harbor master), bought the place in 1932, gave it its nautical name, and transformed it into a restaurant, mostly because Herb's wife liked to cook and was good at it.

It was purchased in 1978 by Philip Tuzi, a born host and a man called the "Toots Shor of Old Town" by writer and ardent Twin Anchors regular Bill Zehme.

"I love no place quite like I love this place. It is everything Chicago is supposed to be: familiar, old, neighborhoody, friendly," wrote Zehme for the restaurant's web site, and though he is no longer a participant in the boozing game, he remains a frequent visitor.

After Phil died, his kids took over, and on any night, you might find Paul Tuzi and his sisters, Mary Kay Cimarusti and Gina Manrique, tending to customers and to the legacy. They love to tell and hear stories about their place, and here is one:

Some years ago, David Mamet was back in his hometown and found himself just wandering around with his wife, Rebecca Pidgeon. He was telling her about his memories of dinners with his late father at a neighborhood saloon that served great ribs.

"And there it was," said Mamet. "Like magic."

AUGUST 26, 2007

'FREE MY DAD'

Ibrahim Parlak's complicated story made a big national noise in March when Chicago writer Alex Kotlowitz detailed his troubling legal battle in the *New York Times Magazine*. Parlak has been in the United States since 1991, when he emigrated from his native Turkey and was granted political asylum. Since 1994, he has owned the popular Middle Eastern restaurant Cafe Gulistan in Harbert, a town in the resort strip that hugs the lake in southwestern Michigan.

Last July, Department of Homeland Security agents arrested Parlak on charges that he committed crimes when he was involved with a Kurdish separatist group in Turkey. The U.S. government has declared him a terrorist and wants him deported. He says he is not a terrorist and wants to stay.

At one of his court appearances in Detroit last December, Parlak's seven-year-old daughter, Livia Gazzolo, stood outside the courtroom wearing a T-shirt that said, FREE MY DAD. (That is Livia, being chased by her father, in happier times.)

Her dad was not freed that day. He remains in jail in Battle Creek, Michigan. Before Kotlowitz's magazine piece, Parlak's story had been detailed in the *Chicago Tribune*, other papers, and on ABC-TV's *Nightline*. This attention was, in great part, the result of Parlak's friends' refusal to let him go quietly to jail. They have been energetic and effective in lobbying reporters (though they have never contacted me) and raising funds for his growing pile of legal bills.

Last September, there was a benefit/reading of the play *Homeland Security* at the Acorn Theater in Three Oaks, near Harbert.

Sidewalks rarely gets into politics, but it has always been the column's aim to introduce you to interesting people and places. We think you should pay close attention to this man and his case.

As Kotlowitz wrote: "Ibrahim Parlak's case is far more than the story of one individual's struggle for freedom. It has dramatic implications for you and the people you know."

MAY 22, 2005

GETTING THEIR DUE

It seems appropriate, if unfortunate, that one of the city's finest permanent art exhibits is buried in the Loop. Just Plain Hardworking sits inside the Msgr. John J. Egan Urban Center on the lower level of DePaul University's Loop Campus, 1 East Jackson Boulevard. "We do get a few people coming in and asking if this is an art gallery," says Linda Levendusky, assistant to the executive director of the Egan center. "But only once in a blue moon."

The exhibit was born when sculptor Margot McMahon began pondering the meaning of celebrity and the city's multiculturalism. It was originally conceived as an exhibition of sculptures. But it expanded into a multimedia show when McMahon enlisted her father, Franklin McMahon, an internationally known artist, to paint portraits of each subject's neighborhood, and got his son (and her brother), William Franklin McMahon, a photojournalist, to do photographic portraits. The Retirement Research Foundation financed the project with a grant that was just enough to cover materials and the publication of a catalog.

Just Plain Hardworking was first seen at the Chicago Historical Society (now the Chicago History Museum) for three months in 1990 and later moved to another downtown location for a few years before finding its current home. It features ten Chicagoans whom McMahon deemed "unsung heroes" from across the city:

Walter Piotrowski, Delois Barrett Campbell (in photo), Frank Drehobl, G. H. Wang, John Egan, Ruth Rothstein, Florence Scala, Frank Lumpkin, Maria Enriquez de Allen, and Hildur Lindquist.

Most have died since the exhibit was created, Scala most recently in August. We could tell you a little about these people, their neighborhoods, their accomplishments, their lives. But we won't. We can't. A couple of sentences don't do them justice. We instead recommend that you visit the exhibit and read the fine biographical essays by James Ylisela.

"[These people] are not the city's most prominent celebrities," Ylisela writes by way of introduction to the exhibit. "Rather, they are a cross section of the men and women who have helped build Chicago."

McMahon is still shadowed by the people she made into art.

"They were remarkable," she says, adding that she spent a great deal of time with each of them. "It was an amazing exhibition to work on, a life-changing experience that has formed many of the paths I follow today. I will go see it a few times a year, mostly when I have visitors from out of town. I think it will tell them something about Chicago that they can't learn anywhere else."

She is absolutely right. Go find this quiet place for quiet heroes.

NOVEMBER 4, 2007

AUTO FOCUS

Jerry Robinson, whom you cannot see but can rest assured is proudly behind the wheel of the car in Osgood's photo, grew up in a small town in northern Minnesota and fell in love with old cars when he was a teenager. "The first one? I was fifteen, and it was a 1948 Chrysler coupe, and the first car I overhauled was a 1941 Packard," he says. "Anything with gears and cams fascinated me. I saw something that moved, and I wanted to know why."

Such inquisitiveness has profoundly influenced his life. It led him to a degree in industrial arts and technology from the University of Minnesota, and to a career as a teacher at Grant Community High School in Fox Lake, not far from his home in Lake Villa. For thirty years he taught, among many things, automotive classes.

He started collecting, and for a time he owned a Ford Model T and other old cars. But the old car he is driving along the quiet country roads around Lake Villa is a Hupmobile he has lovingly cared for and owned for eighteen years.

He is the seventh person to own the automobile, which was purchased new in 1927 for $2,350. By the time Robinson found it for sale from a collector in Genoa, Illinois, it carried a price tag of $6,500.

"It was good to go, but it was the wrong color, had the wrong interior. I brought it back to what it once was," says Robinson, who is now retired from teaching but still quite busy. A member of the Hupmobile Club for almost twenty years, he became its president in 2002, a position he still holds. He is also the editor of the *Hupp Herald*, a thirty-page publication that is put out several times a year and is filled with technical and historical information for those devoted to this little-known vehicle.

"Every collector's got a Ford or a Chrysler. This is different," he says.

The Hupmobile was built from 1909 through 1940 by the Detroit-based Hupp Motor Co., started by Robert Hupp, who had previously worked for Oldsmobile and Ford. In its most successful year, 1926, the company sold sixty-five thousand cars.

Robinson has two Hupmobiles, the one he is driving and a 1925 model that, he admits, "is still a mess. If I can ever stop being the president of the club and editor of the magazine, maybe I'll have time to work on it."

Robinson has been lucky. His wife, Judy, to whom he has been married for forty years, accompanies him on weekly travels along the roads near their home.

"I really love it," she says of the outings, which often include picnics with other Hupmobilers. "I just have a ball."

JULY 29, 2007

HOLLYWOOD'S LOCAL HERO

The Oscars bore me. I have no interest in what outfits the stars, even Cher, are wearing, and I have grown weary, through the years, of the emotionless I'd-so-like-to-thank-my-agent speeches. So, next Sunday night, when the Academy Awards ceremony is broadcast live from Hollywood, I will be reading a book or sleeping or doing the dishes. Still, I will be feeling a bit of pride about this year's event because it has a very strong, if subtle, Chicago connection: This year's Oscar poster is the work of local artist Alex Ross.

Until a few weeks ago, I didn't even know there were special Oscar posters or where one might see or buy one. But hearing that the Wilmette-based Ross was involved made Osgood and me very happy. We've known of Ross and his art for some time. Osgood's son Zac is a comic-book collector and expert, and for years has been touting Ross' work, which compares to the comic-book art of old as a new Jaguar compares to a Model T.

A couple of years ago, the fan and the artist met and became pals. Ross even used Zac as a model for one of the characters in his *Shazam!* books.

Ross is very attuned to local specimens, though he has yet to ask Osgood and me to pose for a new Batman and Robin. He did recently employ the real-life physique of local lovely Rhonda Hampton as the model for the lead character in his book *Wonder Woman: Spirit of Truth.*

In a sense, his Oscar is also modeled on a local "person." For many years the 13½-inch, eight-pound statuettes have been manufactured by the Chicago-based R.S. Owens & Co.

Oregon-born and Texas-raised, Ross came here at seventeen to study painting at the American Academy of Art. Even though he is usually dealing with superheroes, his work is strikingly realistic, a manifestation of his desire to "make heroic figures look real. I think if people can believe such heroes are possible, they might think the good qualities they stand for are also possible."

He practices what he preaches, often auctioning his works to benefit charities such as the Make-a-Wish Foundation, UNICEF, and, earlier this month, the Twin Towers Fund.

Bruce Davis, the executive director of the Academy of Motion Picture Arts and Sciences, is the person who chose Ross to create the poster and is responsible for delivering some fifty thousand of them to theaters, video stores, and sponsors of the awards.

MARCH 17, 2002

NO-NONSENSE EATS

We read about some of the offerings at the hippest of hip new restaurants, Alinea, when *Chicago Tribune* restaurant critic Phil Vettel told us about "a dish that quite literally floats on air. It arrives to the table on an Irish linen pillow filled with lavender-scented air—the weight of the shallow bowl gently forces out the vaporized lavender so it wafts around and above the plate."

We decided to hightail it over to Valois. This is a steam-table cafeteria at 1518 East Fifty-third Street, a Hyde Park gathering spot since 1922. It was opened by a French-Canadian named Valois who surely pronounced his name "Val-wah," and so might be mystified that regulars refer to it as "Val-oise" (as in "noise") or "Val-oy" (as in "toy").

It moved twice before settling into its current location decades ago. It was a favorite of Bill Veeck's and Harold Washington's; was praised by Dawn Simonds, restaurant critic for *Cincinnati* magazine, in her 2004 book, *Best Food in Town: The Restaurant Lover's Guide to Comfort Food*

in the Midwest; and was the setting for Mitch Duneier's remarkable sociological study, *Slim's Table*.

But it has withstood these periodic flings with fame to remain a no-nonsense spot with a charmingly direct slogan, "See Your Food."

What you see is corned beef and cabbage, roast beef, short ribs, butt steak, all manner of breakfast foods; generous portions, accompanied by bowls of vegetables, hot corn bread, and grits. And the prices: You could feed a family of four here for what you might pay for an appetizer at one of the city's chic culinary playgrounds.

The clientele is an encouraging mix of neighborhood families, University of Chicago students, cops, cabbies, retirees, black and white, and everything in between.

The place is, as *Chicago Tribune* writer Ron Grossman put it many years ago, "a Noah's Ark of human diversity." Lines can get long at peak hours, but some people eat three meals a day at the place, and others spend hours lingering over coffee and conversation. These people are just fine not knowing anything about vaporized lavender.

OCTOBER 9, 2005

COLUMN ABOUT A COLUMN

They whiz by, on bikes and skates and running shoes, on their way to who knows where, but fully unaware of the history that sits just off their determined path. There it is, in Osgood's photo, a majestic column, a two-thousand-year-old relic that few even notice. It may live in the memories of old minds still sharp enough to remember it, on prominent display, in front of the Italian Pavilion at the Century of Progress International Exposition, a world's fair in 1933. But there were so many other "delights"—futuristic cars and homes; and more dubiously, a "Midget City" featuring sixty Lilliputians, incubators that contained real babies; and the legendary fan dancing of Sally Rand—that a person could forget about a column.

It was brought to our attention (we are not big on biking, skating, or running) by Lynn Hauldren, who wrote to us, the old-fashioned way: "I was amazed to find [the column] there. Had never heard of it in all my years in Chicago..." He offered the opinion that "[it] has to be the oldest man-made object in Chicago."

We always check such historical matters with our friend Tim Samuelson, the cultural historian of the city. He says, "In New York City there's the so-called Cleopatra's Needle, in Central Park, which dates from 1450 BC. There are probably lots of other ancient artifacts transplanted around the country too.

"But I can't think of anything older, in Chicago, standing outside in a public place. Can't be 100 percent sure on this, but there's a good likelihood that the Balbo column is oldest. I know there are some older items right on the exterior of Tribune Tower courtesy of the Colonel [former *Chicago Tribune* owner Col. Robert R. McCormick]." (And, yes, some of the rocks embedded in this building are older than the column.)

The column came from a portico on the beach at Ostia, the port of Imperial Rome, and was presented to Chicago in honor of General Italo Balbo, who in 1933 led a flock of twenty-four seaplanes here. Yes, Balbo, who helped bring Mussolini to power. It was this Fascist publicity stunt that resulted in his name being permanently, and sadly, slapped on what once was Seventh Street.

Perhaps it would be better to have a street named for Hauldren.

You may not know his name but you have certainly seen and heard him. He was the advertising copywriter who became the Empire Carpet Man in the 1970s when, legend has it, a professional actor didn't show up for a commercial and he filled the role.

He became a decades-long advertising icon, the person who wrote the jingle that accompanies the company's famous phone number, and delivered it with style: "Five-eight-eight-two-three-hundred...Empire." He is a clever guy, who lives in Evanston. In his letter he suggested, irresistibly, "Hey, a column about a column!"

JUNE 7, 2009

COUNTER SPY

For many decades there were a large number of Midwestern bars and restaurants (and bar/restaurants) that tried, with various aggressive methods, to entertain their customers in ways that food and alcohol could not. These places had a profound effect on *New Yorker* writer A. J. Liebling when he came here for extended stays in the late 1940s; trips that resulted in articles for the magazine that coined our "Second City" nickname and contained this observation:

> A thing about Chicago that impressed me from the hour I got there was the saloon. New York bars operate on the principle that you want a drink or you wouldn't be there…Chicago bars assume that nobody likes liquor, and that to induce the customers to purchase even a minute quantity, they have to provide a show.

Few such places survive in our town today, but there may not be a more durable example of the ilk than the Safe House in Milwaukee. It opened in 1966 and remains as lively-goofy and enjoyable as ever. It's all about spies and espionage and its theme is pleasantly hammered home, from the decor (check your coat in the Cloak and Dagger Room) to the menu (try the Spy Burger and, for dessert, Bond's Bomb).

Playing along, it would not be fair to divulge too many of its many delights.

Its location? You won't see any sign, but head to the "offices" of International Exports Ltd., 779 North Front Street, near City Hall.

New diversions are always being created or added. Among the latest is a cell door from the infamous Hohenschoenhausen prison, run by East Germany's Stasi secret police.

Grim as that may be, we admire the sense of history.

This is also manifest in the Centennial 1908–2008 Great Race. This auto race begins May 30 in New York City and heads west toward a Paris finish, scheduled for August 2. (The cars will deal with that tricky Pacific Ocean by being flown from Vancouver to Shanghai). One of the cars is that of Dr. Rich McKone of Peoria. He'll act as navigator while Jerry Price, of Plymouth, Wisconsin, serves as driver/mechanic.

The Safe House connection?

Well, the car is a converted 1967 Aston Martin DB6.

Aston Martin. James Bond. Get it?

The Safe House is sponsoring the car and will track its progress on the large map behind its Interpol bar. Owner David Baldwin, seen in Osgood's photo, says that no matter the race's outcome, there will be a "victory party" at the bar/restaurant. It should be jammed.

APRIL 27, 2008

ACHTUNG, BABY!

It is easy to feel, walking down many busy city streets, that the world has become a dull and homogenized place. Yes, there is a Starbucks on the southwest corner of Belmont Avenue and Clark Street. And on the blocks heading west from there are such ubiquitous urban oases as Jamba Juice and Potbelly. And the Quiet Knight, the legendary music club on the second floor of a building hard by the "L" has long been gone, replaced by a hair salon and tanning parlor. And the street life is not as wild and weird and wonderful as it once was.

But you can still get a tattoo or a piercing on this Belmont strip (roughly from Halsted Street to Sheffield Avenue). You can stop into the J. Toguri Mercantile store for gifts you're unlikely to find anywhere else; visit the venerable Alley, forty thousand square feet of "the biggest and the best selections in rock, biker, punk, mod, emo, rockabilly, and gothic shoes and clothing;" and a great

deal more. You can drop into a nice bookstore, stay in a hotel, eat cinnamon rolls at Ann Sather, and go to Berlin.

It has been twenty-five years since this club opened at 954 West Belmont Avenue and, in its way, helped change the way the city partied. At the time, there were few places hospitable to both gay and straight crowds, but here they mingled comfortably, creating a mix energetic almost beyond words.

The place started as a video bar, taking advantage of the wares of the recently launched MTV. It became home to all manner of clever and crazy art installations and events. I have some vague memories of being there for a Tammy Faye Bakker look-alike contest and one, perhaps two, spaghetti wrestling matches. I never did make it to the club's anti-New Year's Eve party and, since my late nights of music and dancing have become ruefully infrequent, hadn't been there in a while.

Osgood had never been there until recently, shooting photos of Shania Van Selus watching a performance by Bunny Rabbit, also known as Mother Miracle, late one night.

"It's amazing. Why hadn't I been there?" he says. "The real action seems to start at 2:00 AM. That's not exactly my liveliest hour, but I am so glad I was there. I expected it to be dark and weird, but it was wild and fun and silly, with people dressed in various outlandish attire. I had a blast."

Many, many years ago, a patron of the original Billy Goat Tavern, across the street from the old Chicago Stadium, referred to it as "a perpetual Halloween." That's also true of Berlin. Though not enough clubs followed its pioneering path, it remains a vital, colorful, and important institution on a street that still sizzles in a world growing ever gray.

JULY 8, 2007

THE SPIRIT(S) OF CHICAGO

We are all haunted. It might be by a person or a place or a thing, but each of us has something that shadows our days and nights. Norman Maclean, the late University of Chicago professor, let us know what it was for him when he concluded his majestic novella, *A River Runs Through It*, with these sentences:

> Eventually, all things merge into one, and a river runs through it. The river was cut by the world's great flood and runs over rocks from the basement of time. On some of the rocks are timeless raindrops. Under the rocks are the words, and some of the words are theirs. I am haunted by waters.

Ursula Bielski has devoted her life to ghosts. She has written books about ghosts and cemeteries, all richly detailed and embellished with history and a sure sense of place, which is Chicago. Along with her husband, writer David Cowan, she operates Chicago Hauntings tours.

The ghost that most haunts Bielski is that of Mary Bregovy, who was a young woman when she died in 1934 and who is known as Resurrection Mary, for the southwest suburban cemetery in which she was buried.

There is debate about whether this woman is the real deal; some ghostfolk believe Mary is the spirit of one or another dead girl. But, for Bielski, Bregovy is it. It is her ghost that is "seen" wandering near the cemetery, sometimes trying to get into the cars of those driving on Archer Avenue.

"I wake up in the middle of the night and wonder how I will ever bring Mary Bregovy's story to the audience she deserves," Bielski says. "She is pure Chicago, and tells our whole tale lushly and elegantly at once. If you can't find Chicago in Mary's story, then Chicago is surely lost."

The latest chapter of the story came not long ago, when Bielski was driving past the Satala Funeral Home, 4611 South Damen Avenue, and noticed a for-sale sign.

"This was where Mary's body was prepared," she says. "And the whole Back of the Yards neighborhood represents everything that I do. I drive around it and think about the fact that Mary, the daughter of Polish immigrants, walked through it each morning to Packingtown to go to work, and that today it is home to an entirely different generation of immigrants that is, as was Mary, trying to get out. "I've spent so many years trying to bring home the larger meaning of these ghost stories. Still, I never felt that the story of Mary has been brought to as wide an audience as it needs to be. She means so much more than people realize."

Perhaps one day Bielski will tell that story in a book. That will have to wait. This is the busy season for those in the ghost business and a fine time to ask what, or who, is haunting you.

OCTOBER 7, 2007

CHICAGO'S GOT TALENT

There is no twenty-one-year-old alive who has spent more time in saloons, nightclubs, and show lounges than Dakota Horvath and, remarkably, he is none the worse for the wee-hour wear. He recently returned from Las Vegas, where he performed *The Songs of Bobby Darin* in the showroom at the South Point Casino on the Strip, and immediately popped into a West Loop recording studio to put the finishing touches on his new CD. Still relatively unknown, he is a singer of great talent and serious ambitions.

"There's a lot I want to do with my music," he says. "It really is my life. I was surrounded by it from the time I can first remember. I was singing when I was two."

His parents played music in the Northwest Side house in which he grew up as one of three kids, and his grandfather had been a bass player at the legendary Chez Paree nightclub in the 1930s and '40s.

His hero forever has been Frank Sinatra. Horvath's first public performance took place when he was five, at a Miami club owned by actor Mickey Rourke. He sang "My Way."

Horvath subsequently built a resume bursting with the big names with whom he has shared a stage (Don Rickles, Natalie Cole, Trisha Yearwood, Tony Bennett), nearly eighty television appearances, and such high-profile gigs as singing at the 2000 wedding of Brad Pitt and Jennifer Aniston.

For most of these events he was viewed more as novelty than talent: *Oh, look, a little kid doing Sinatra!* He was okay with this for a time. He was a kid, doing other kid things such as going to high school at Luther North and competing in the Golden Gloves. But he also began sneaking into such places as Lonie Walker's Underground Wonderbar and other local clubs.

"I just wanted to listen," he says. "And most of the owners indulged me."

Like any other young performer, he was a sponge. In addition to Sinatra, he cites as influences a crowd that includes Stevie Wonder, Billie Holiday, Sting, Gino Vanelli, and Chicago's own Kurt Elling.

"I really started to get serious about having a career when I was about fifteen," he says. "To be really honest, I was not a big fan of school."

Managed now by Barb Bailey, he has been playing around town, at such places as the Supper Club in the Seneca Hotel, Philander's in Oak Park, Andy's Jazz Club, and Katerina's, good and respected venues all.

He writes an increasing amount of original material, reckons that he might retire from performing in fifteen years, and perhaps then direct and write scores for films. He might open a nightclub, which he would call Dakota's. First things first, though. He wants his own place. He is still living with his folks

JUNE 14, 2009

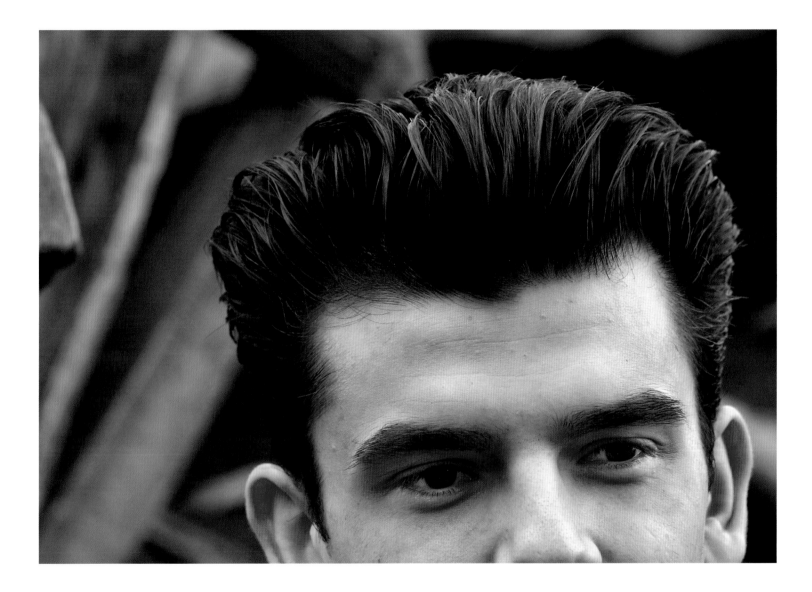

HALL OF LEARNING

A few computers are scattered about the 11,632 square feet of the George Cleveland Hall branch of the Chicago Public Library, but this remains a place of books and words and quiet dreams. Versie Barnes, head librarian at Hall, is a pleasant woman who feels the weight of the building's history, however shadowy it might now be to others who never visit this neglected corner of the city. "It is personally special to be here," said Barnes, who has worked in the library system for twenty-three years and has headed Hall since September 1997.

This building would be an eye-catcher in any part of the city. But here, at Forthy-eighth Street and Michigan Avenue, a few bleak blocks east of the Robert Taylor Homes and surrounded by empty lots and tattered apartment buildings, it looks especially out of place.

The neighborhood is called Grand Boulevard and in the 1920s the area was at the hub of the vibrant enclave called Bronzeville, full of shops and clubs and hopes. One thing it lacked—which every African-American neighborhood in Chicago lacked— was a library. A prominent African-American physician named George Cleveland Hall convinced philanthropist Julius Rosenwald of the need for a library in the community. Rosenwald, who headed Sears, Roebuck and Co. and had financed the building of the nearby Michigan Boulevard Garden Apartments, bought the land at Forty-eighth and Michigan and gave it to the city.

Built of Indiana limestone in the Italian Renaissance style, it features an octagonal rotunda with terrazzo tile, brass ornaments, and dark English oak. It opened January 18, 1932, and its first head librarian was also the city's first African-American librarian, the now-revered Vivian G. Harsh.

At Hall, Harsh began to amass the Special Negro Collection: books, pamphlets, newspaper clippings, photos, and whatever else she could get her hands on. It was a sad sign of those times that Andrew J. Kolar, then president of the city library board of directors, argued that the books Harsh "was installing in the new Hall branch were likely to cause a race riot."

In 1970, the collection was renamed the Vivian G. Harsh Research Collection of Afro-American History and Literature. Since 1975, it has been housed at the Carter G. Woodson Regional Library, 9525 South Halsted Street. With tens of thousands of items, it is the largest African-American history collection in the Midwest.

"This is a very poor area, and we have to meet its needs," Barnes said.

A seven-year-old boy named Kevin looked at a book of animal photos and said, "This is my special place. I like it more than school."

A group of kids came in from the cold, filled with after-school giggles.

"Sssshhh," said Barnes, gently. "You're in a library."

The kids hushed and streamed purposefully into rooms filled with books. They seemed to know exactly where they were, and were glad to be there.

FEBRUARY 21, 1999

A VETERAN OF LIFE

In the twenty-some years I have known Chuck Lofrano, I have never heard him complain, though he has more right than almost anyone I know to bitch about the tough breaks he's had. He is a South Sider by birth and by disposition, a Roseland kid who did all the good and bad things kids did growing up in the 1950s and '60s. He palled around with such guys as Dennis DeYoung, who would go on to form and lead the band Styx. He fell in love with, and would marry, Pamela Feusi, one of four legendarily beautiful South Side sisters, rivaled, perhaps, only by the three Rago girls, among them Suzanne, who became DeYoung's wife.

Then came, as it did for so many young men at the time, Vietnam. That is him now, in Osgood's photo, holding a 1968 snapshot of himself (left) and some buddies in Vietnam. As an infantry machine gunner with the Marines, he lived and fought with "a fear that was always with me." That fear was replaced by agony when his left arm was all but blown off his body during a jungle firefight.

That is all captured in a book, *In Spite of It All*, a remarkably honest and surprisingly hopeful memoir. It is hard to imagine how difficult it must have been for him to relive, in print, coming home to a series of hospitals and operations, the "uneasy truce with our fellow countrymen" he and other veterans felt, and the difficulties of assimilation.

Less taxing was detailing success as a salesman in the information-technology business, and his wife's loyalty and love, and that of their three daughters. But then come the miseries of four heart attacks, quadruple-bypass surgery, and a kidney transplant, the organ coming from daughter Lisa. Through it all, he remains determined to "find a way to overcome obstacles…to fight for the happiness and goodness that is ours to claim."

The centerpiece of the book concerns his involvement as one of the organizers of the Vietnam veterans "Welcome Home" parade June 13, 1986, in Chicago. It attracted two hundred thousand marchers and was followed by a Petrillo Music Shell concert that featured DeYoung. He sang a new song that had been inspired by Lofrano. It was called "Black Wall" and contained these lyrics:

> They won every battle they fought
> But the one that raged at home
> And now the only words that count
> Are the names carved out in stone
> As tears fall onto stone.

Tuesday is Veterans Day. Lofrano, as usual, will celebrate at home with his family and then get together with some other veterans. That's his low-key way. In the book, he writes, "I do not wish to present myself as an extraordinary person or as a hero."

Sorry, but by any definition, he is both.

NOVEMBER 9, 2008

YOUTH MOVEMENT

It is early on a cold Saturday morning. Winter hangs on hard and gray snow is pasted to patches of ground that, soon enough, will be green with grass. One by one they start to arrive, a dozen tiny children. Some of them come on foot and a couple, regally, in strollers. A few are cradled in a mother's or father's arms.

Most are girls. One is a boy. Once inside the Hyde Park Neighborhood Club, they begin to shed their coats and hats and boots and scarves and emerge a pack of pink. The boy is not wearing pink. "I'm a ballerina," says one and then another and another. The boy does not say this. There are many activities going on in this building. There are organized basketball games, filled with exuberant teenagers. There are gentle-looking exercise classes for those no longer limber of limb. A few people can be seen on blue floor mats in a room with the lights low—yoga, it appears.

For most of the winter and into the spring the little ballerinas, and the boy, have been part of one of the many classes that comprise the "curriculum" of the Hyde Park School of Dance. Their Creative Movement class is formally described as "exploration of dance movement with the use of imagery, such as dancing elephants and beautiful butterflies, as inspiration." None of them is able to read that description.

"I'm a bee," says one, hopping about the studio, and then another and another: "I'm a bee."

We are there on the one Saturday parents and other kin and friends are allowed to observe the thirty-minute class. The studio's walls are lined with people whose faces are stuck in smiles and whose eyes peer through video or still cameras. Among the faces are those of Kurt and Jennifer Elling; he the great jazz singer just back from touring in Asia, she a former professional ballet dancer and still a teacher, and they, together, the parents of the youngest dancer in class, Luiza Jade, not yet three.

"We are so fortunate to have the school thriving here on the South Side," says Jennifer Elling. "I have taught here on and off over the years. It's a beautiful experience watching and helping young dancers grow. I realize even more how important the school is now that Luiza is here."

The woman teaching the Creative Movement class is August Tye. She is the founder and artistic director of the school. When it started in 1993, she was its only teacher. There were thirty students. Currently there are ten faculty members and more than three hundred students. Tye has a wonderful career in dance. She was a member of the Joel Hall Dancers, Salt Creek Ballet, and Second City Ballet. She works with the Lyric Opera, most recently as the revival choreographer for its production of *Eugene Onegin*. She is married to an opera singer and the couple has

two daughters, ages four and eight, who are students at Mom's school. Tye teaches as many as fifteen classes a week, for kids of all ages and adults, but she finds a special pleasure in her littlest dancers.

"There is a great joy in the natural creativity kids have at this age. I guide them, experiment with movement," she says. "I see their confidence being built. I see them having a great time. I see all those perfectly limber little bodies falling in love with dance."

But there are so many things in which to fall in love in the tender years—a cloud, a leaf, or a color. And so, not far from the dance studio, we are in a room that, again, is a mess.

It has been this way every Tuesday for the last couple of months, when it has been occupied for ninety minutes by six kids between the freewheeling ages of three and five. And so, on this day, one little girl has glued a couple of fingers together. Another has drawn a large "F" on her hand.

"I want a pink balloon," says one of these pint-sized Picassos, though the day's project, a Halloween mask, wouldn't seem to call for such an item.

Pinned to the walls of this classroom at the Hyde Park Art Center are works by older kids and, if one was to make quick judgment, these would be deemed more accomplished. But it is in this Discover Art class that one gets a vivid reminder of the unbridled creativity of kids.

The class is one of dozens offered at the Hyde Park Art Center for children and adults. The teacher is a young woman of great imagination and admirable patience named Sara Holwerda. There she is in Osgood's photo, holding an item made by one of the older kids.

"My dad is a painter, and I have always had access to art supplies and grew up with the idea that being creative was a daily activity," she says. "My dad taught me a few things directly, but mostly I hung out around his studio. Sometimes I'd entertain myself with puppet shows."

After graduating from the University of Michigan School of Art and Design, she moved to Chicago in 2006 and started teaching at the Hyde Park Art Center. "I teach summer camps, workshops, and a few adult classes, including Acrylic Painting and Creative Process. Creative Process is sort of an interdisciplinary workshop where we work on creativity and do things to be more prolific and think more freely...like children."

HIZZONER

The mayor of the City of Chicago is Richard J. Daley, as embodied by Neil Giuntoli, the author and star of *Hizzoner*. This is a play that sprouted at the Prop Thtr in 2006 and has since entertained and, in many cases, haunted audiences at various locations ever since. "How many performances? I've lost count, but somewhere between 350 to 380," Giuntoli says. "There are three reasons I haven't grown weary of the role. First, the play itself, which is fun to perform. Secondly, the audiences. They keep me going. The relationship with them is mystical and divine. Lastly, I have the best production team and cast any guy could ever hope for. They are family."

As a young actor here decades ago, Giuntoli performed in such original works as *The Crate Dweller*—about a Nazi-freak Vietnam veteran living in a cardboard box—before being lured to Hollywood, where he fashioned a successful career in more than fifty movies and TV shows.

But Daley was always with him.

"He was every Chicagoan's secret dad, and they miss him, as they miss those days long gone by," he says. "People want to drink from the fountain of their youth."

Beginning in Daley's doctor's office on December 20, 1976, the day of his death (also, spookily, Giuntoli's birthday), the play travels back in time and place. Set mainly in the mayor's office on the fifth floor of City Hall, it focuses on Dr. Martin Luther King Jr.'s 1968 assassination and the Democratic convention later that year.

Critics have raved. Others too. Robert Hanley, a retired Chicago police officer who was a member of the bodyguard detail for the mayor from 1967 to 1971, was moved close to tears by Giuntoli's performance. "You got it down pat, my man," he told the actor.

This sort of reaction, times hundreds, has convinced Giuntoli and some film and television producers that there is life for *Hizzoner* beyond Chicago stages. But it has not tempted Giuntoli to enter politics.

"I realize the extraordinary resolve and determination that our current mayor has to possess to even board the elevator to the fifth floor, every day," he says. "My hat's off to him. I get to slip out of the suit after a two-hour show and go back to being Neil Giuntoli."

Our current mayor has not seen *Hizzoner* but John Kass has. There may be no more energetic and articulate critic of the mayor than Kass, who is not often given credit for his gifts as a theater critic. This is what he wrote after seeing the play: "If you love Chicago, if you've ever called yourself a Chicagoan, then do yourself a favor and see *Hizzoner*, the remarkable play about the city's dead king."

MARCH 22, 2009

HIPSO FACTO

The man in Osgood's photo, peering through one of those old-fashioned gizmos once used for eye tests, is Brandon Nelson, and he is yet another of the creative characters who call Three Oaks, Michigan, home. A native of St. Charles, he first visited southwest Michigan in 1995, taking a first-wedding-anniversary trip from Chicago with his wife, Lisa. She and her family had been vacationing in the area for generations. Indeed, her parents had a house there, and although the young couple was in the process of digging up the dough to buy the three-flat in which they had been living in Wicker Park, they fell in love with a house in the town of Sawyer.

"Buy it? It would be a risk, an immediate change in our plans and in our lives," said Nelson.

Without jobs in the area or any idea of what work they might be able to find, they took the leap. Nelson had a background in art (he graduated from the School of the Art Institute and was an apprentice to the late Chicago sculptor Eldon Danhausen) and music (he played drums with the rock-fusion band Disarray). He was also a collector of "odd items," he said, "starting with stuff I found in my grandmother's hot, musty attic."

He got a job with Lakeside Antiques, eventually taking part of the store's space to sell his own things and many more that he found at house and estate sales.

His business began to grow, and so, in 2002, he took another leap, leasing a former video store/tanning parlor that had been vacant for a year in Three Oaks. He named it Ipso Facto, and in it he displays an ever-changing array of antiques, art, and, it's fair to say, curiosities and oddities.

"I don't specialize in anything," he said. "I trust my response to the things I see, and I love strange stuff that I've never seen before, physical fragments of history."

Lucinda Hahn knows Ipso Facto. She is a more recent transplant to the area, a former *Chicago Tribune* staff writer who has been editor, for the past year, of *Lake Magazine*, which covers all things southwest Michigan and places nearby.

"It's a great store and fits in nicely with what I think of as the funky feel of Three Oaks," she said. "It's such a tiny little town, and it's not terribly polished or done up, which is nice. It's just casual and, yes, funky. But it's packed full of offbeat stuff of very high quality."

She went on to mention all sorts of things, including the organic soup at Froehlich's, the movies at Vickers Theatre, B Books, and the live performances at the Acorn Theater.

"I love it up here," said Nelson. "We took a risk, and we have been able to make a good life." He and his wife are now raising two young daughters, and he also has a new band, an electronic folk group named Squirm Orchestra, whose musicians are all from the area.

JULY 15, 2007

"SING US A SONG TONIGHT . . . '

The names of most of the bars in which Dave Green has played the piano are beyond recall now. Long-vanished, they can only be conjured in faded news clips or foggy memories. Does anyone remember Yvette or Christopher's or Toulouse or Palette's? He's played them all, and so many more. He's been at this for half a century, after giving up a short career as a boxer that saw him climb into the ring in small-town joints for nearly seventy bouts. Thank the musical gods that those fights did nothing to damage his hands, for they went on to give so much pleasure and solace to those who sat next to his piano late into the night.

Though there are still a number of piano bars around, they are an endangered species. Witness the recent remodeling that removed Judy Roberts, one of the relatively few females to ply the piano-bar trade, from her corner of the InterContinental Hotel (so marvelously close to the *Chicago Tribune*) and transformed the room into some sort of wine-chocolate-cheese experience called Eno.

Judy is now at the Coq d'Or on Thursday, Friday, and Saturday nights.

Dave doesn't have a regular gig these days, but he's around.

Osgood captured him with his ever-present smile and hat, playing at a January breakfast in honor of Rev. Martin Luther King Jr. at the Chicago Hilton and Towers.

Entertainment such as this—live music in hotels or restaurants—is part of an ancient local tradition, dating to that ebullient early settler Mark Beaubien, who enlivened his Sauganash Inn with fine fiddle playing and lusty ballads in the 1830s.

Piano bars have always been places of smoky shadows, high hopes, and broken hearts. "It's a quarter to three . . ." and all that. But shelter was to be found, provided by people like Dave and Judy. So if you can find a good piano bar, pull up a seat. The closer the better.

FEBRUARY 25, 2007

FAMILY VENUES

The face in Osgood's photo is Mike Leonard's face, and it has been on national television for the twenty-six years he has been a correspondent for the *Today* show on NBC. "Some people say, 'I've never seen you,' 'I've never heard of you,' and that's fine," says Leonard. "I never hang out with the TV types. I live in a satellite world because it's better for me and for my family that way. I don't want to live in that celebrity world."

Leonard, born in Paterson, New Jersey, in 1947, was raised in Glencoe. He and his wife, Cathy, live in Winnetka, where they raised four children.

"When I was teenager, I was really lousy in school, not at all creative, shy," he says. "Then I saw a Bob Dylan concert at Ravinia, and everything changed. His lyrics touched me, and it was the first time I ever valued words. I decided at the time that I would be a creative person. I thought that was my destiny. I just didn't know how."

For many years, his only creative outlet was making home movies.

"For seven or eight years, as I got married and started having kids and was working construction and some mindless jobs, I used that camera. I have always felt that life moves too quickly. This was my way of slowing it down. I would focus on the little moments, the ordinary things: my daughter running to a school bus, my son reading in a chair."

He and his family were living in Phoenix when, on the suggestion of a friend, he took his home movies to local TV stations.

"I'm thirty years old, I've got this broken nose, no journalism degree, not a smooth talker," he says. "I got rejected by all the stations until this guy at PBS took pity on me and paid me out of petty cash to do some stories."

Three months later, he was hired as a sportscaster at another station, and not long after that he was spotted by a *Today* show producer and offered a network job. His *Today* show pieces are always described as "quirky." "I don't know why people use that word," he says. "What I do is the stuff that happens every day."

Among the most memorable "stuff" is a trip he took with his family and his parents.

"My parents were getting old, and one morning I just woke up and I told my wife, 'I'm going to get an RV and give my parents one last lap around the country.' I don't know why I thought RV. I'd never even been in a RV. I called *Today* and asked to have a month off. Once we got on the road, I started to see this as a good story. I did a four-part series for the show and was asked by an agent if I'd like to write a book."

The result is *The Ride of Our Lives: Roadside Lessons of an American Family*, a charming, funny, not-so-funny, and altogether honest tale that should put a smile on any reader's face.

AUGUST 5, 2007

AUDUBON ON THE AVENUE

It's hard to imagine what kind of person Joel Oppenheimer might be if he had spent his working life standing over a punch press. But being lucky enough to have enjoyed a career surrounded by beauty, he remains passionate about his profession. He owns the Oppenheimer Gallery, which sits on street level in the north section of the Wrigley Building. This is a conspicuous space, but thousands of people still pass it every day without ever thinking of going inside.

"We are so specialized that we don't get the same crowds that line up for [Garrett's] popcorn," says Oppenheimer.

His gallery is internationally known, and visitors are drawn by the work of the many artists on exhibit, but mostly by a superstar named John James Audubon, who is, without argument, the most famous nature artist of his time (1785–1851), or anybody else's.

"The Audubon images have become ubiquitous," Oppenheimer says. "They are on place mats, coffee cups. His art has suffered from that kind of exposure, become a victim of its own popularity. But to walk in here and see the real thing, well, seeing the real thing just opens your eyes."

He is right. The Audubon images that cover the walls are striking in their composition and color and size and, for city folk, their novelty. Many of us will never see a great horned owl, Arctic tern, or white heron in the feathered flesh, but these representations more than suffice.

When you visit, and you should (though many works are out of the price range of most of us, some small works are priced reasonably enough for you to start your own collection), do not look past the gallery's other artists, including Margaret Mee (1909–1988) and her orchids and other flora of the Amazon, or Maria Sibylla Merian (1647–1717) and her flowers and butterflies. The most colorful of these will put those of a certain age in mind of the best psychedelic art.

Oppenheimer, holding one of Audubon's birds in Osgood's photo, studied art history and painting at the School of the Art Institute. He took a part-time job with Douglas Kenyon, then running a gallery that dealt primarily in photography. Eventually the two got hooked, so to speak, on Audubon and became partners. In 1992, Oppenheimer bought his partner out, and in 1997 opened his Wrigley Building gallery.

He now also has a gallery in Charleston, South Carolina. He runs a conservation, restoration, and framing operation. He is a publisher, producing rare, limited-edition prints as well as magnificent and massive books in collaboration with the Field Museum, the New York Historical Society, and the Royal Botanic Gardens at Kew. The Wrigley Building gallery also contains what might be the city's most unusual bookstore; where else can you pick up a copy of George Brookshaw's *Pomona Britannica*?

"Isn't this just beautiful?" says Oppenheimer, and it's difficult to know if he means the book on his lap, the painting on the wall, or, lucky man, his own life.

SEPTEMBER 30, 2007

DOWNSTATE HOSPITALITY

Xenia is some two hundred fifty miles southwest of Chicago, as the crow flies. It seems a bit further with Osgood behind the wheel, but it's worth a visit, especially if you happen to be in such nearby towns as Effingham, Salem, and Mt. Vernon, or in that big city, St. Louis, due west. The origin of the town's name is now firmly buried under the dust of history. Some people think it was named for Xenia, Ohio. Another story has it that a visiting preacher, impressed with the kindnesses encountered during a tavern visit, suggested the place be named for the Greek word for hospitality.

Osgood and I prefer the theory that because this area is so beautiful—Xenia's slogan is "Garden Spot of the World"—some learned townsfolk named it for Princess Xenia of Greece.

In any case, it is the only municipality in the state beginning with the letter X. It has four hundred-some residents, people like Tina Golden and her ten-year-old daughter Hannah, in Osgood's photo. Tina is Xenia's secretary/treasurer, and what she's holding in her hand while standing on Front Street is a rare item.

So infrequently does a town's ZIP code correspond to a specific date, that when such a thing took place here on June 28, 1999 (6/28/99), the U.S. Postal Service deemed the occasion worthy of celebration with a ZIP Code Day designation.

The Goldens are proud of that and they don't have a great deal of interest in the big 606 ZIPs to the northeast. Tina has been to Chicago three times, she told Osgood, and didn't feel comfortable on any of those trips.

But she plans to come back one day soon with Hannah and the other child she has adopted. She wants them to visit the city in which they were born. We hope they have a nice time.

And if you should see them, try to show them some Chicago hospitality.

DECEMBER 14, 2003

BLAGO'S MANE MAN

Once every three weeks, former governor Rod Blagojevich rides a tiny elevator to the sixth floor of an unremarkable building on one of the city's chicest blocks. There he sits in the same fake leather chair, one of four chairs at Mr. Barber on Oak, as a Soviet immigrant named Peter Vodovoz spends twenty minutes tending to what is the most famous haircut in the world. "He has always been a super guy to me," says Vodovoz. "Yes, he has a lot of hair, but cutting it is easy."

He has been cutting that hair for more than a decade, beginning when Blagojevich was a populist Democratic congressman with ambitions for national office and a hairdo that was of modest interest. The hair became the object of loud and widespread ridicule in the wake of Blagojevich's December 9 arrest, January 29 impeachment, and April 2 indictment on sixteen racketeering, fraud, and extortion counts.

"Some of the talk has been disturbing to me and not any of it has been funny," says Vodovoz. "This is a man who was elected by so many people (1.8 million in 2002 and more than 1.6 million in his 2006 reelection) that he deserves better until his situation is finished in the courts."

As energetically as Blagojevich has courted media attention, Vodovoz has avoided it.

"There are many, many people who call and come in here looking for information about Rod," he says. "What does he talk about? Does he have secret meetings here? I have been offered money to talk to these people. I have been offered money for pieces of Rod's hair. I turn all of this down, because I have respect for my customers.

"My customers have a right to know I don't talk about them behind their backs," he says.

That's an admirable trait in an age in which people are willing, even eager, to share the particulars of their encounters with celebrities or newsmakers, no matter how trivial, tangential, or insipid: Yes, I'll never forget the time Drew Petersen talked to me at a local restaurant. What was the conversation? Well, he asked me to pass the ketchup.

Another reason for Vodovoz's public silence was that he felt no need to defend his handiwork.

"For me it is a simple thing. A man walks in and asks to have his hair cut a certain way, who am I to tell him different?" he says. "You do not walk into a bar and order a beer and have the bartender say, 'No, no, you should have a scotch.' You tell me what kind of hair cut you want, you get that kind of hair cut."

Vodovoz was born in Mogilev-Podolsky, a city of forty thousand in the Ukraine. The youngest of six boys, his mother died when he was two and he and his brothers were raised by their father Yakov, a former boxer and World War II veteran, who worked long hours as a tailor.

A talented folk dancer, he graduated from the Kiev State Institute of Culture. But arts jobs were scarce and so, after serving two years in the Russian army, he learned the barbering trade.

He emigrated in 1989, arriving in Chicago with $1 in his pocket, eventually cutting hair and giving shaves at the Drake Hotel barbershop. In 2000 he opened Mr. Barber on Oak. The shop's claim/motto is "We Make You Handsome" but it would be a mistake to let its tony address, 67 East Oak Street, fool you. This is no fancy salon. It is a barber shop.

Vodovoz has built a long list of loyal clients that includes some big names from the worlds of sports, business, and politics. There are only a few photos on the shop's walls, most of them athletes. There is no photo of former secretary of commerce and brother of the city's mayor, Bill Daley. Nor is there one of Blagojevich.

He shares his shop with another barber/business partner, Helen Kashper, and with an affable shoeshine man, Billy Hill. He works seven days a week, taking the train back and forth from Vernon Hills. There he lives with his wife of fourteen years, Stella. She was a refugee from a war-torn Azerbijan, where she had worked as a hair stylist. The couple met at a birthday party for his friend and her brother, Vladimir.

The couple has a bright and personable nine-year-old daughter named Emily, whose morning and late afternoon training sessions at a local pool attest to her ambition to be "a swimmer in the Olympics, especially when they are in Chicago."

Since he has, until now, refused all requests for interviews, his name has surfaced only once in the media. It was during Blagojevich's June 3, 2009 appearance on *Larry King Live* on CNN.

King said, "They tell me thousands of people want to know who cuts [your hair]..."

Blagojevich responded, "I want to plug my barber. His name is Peter, Mr. Barber on Oak. He's a great guy. He cuts Lou Piniella's hair and Mick Jagger actually went to his barber shop when he was here for a concert. I know people make fun of it. Whatever they say, it is what it is."

The bond between barber and customer is an enduring one, the shop a shelter of sorts. You find someone who does right by your hair and knows when to keep his or her mouth shut, you stick with them for keeps, through marriages and hangovers, through all of life's ups and downs.

Recently Blagojevich, after paying for his $35 haircut with a personal check, inscribed a photo and gave it to Vodovoz.

It reads, "To the best barber an ex-governor could ever have."

LOOK! UP IN THE AIR!

It may be comforting to know that your children will not have to run away to join the circus. That's because there is, and has been for five years, a circus troupe based permanently in Chicago. The Midnight Circus is one of the city's lesser known treasures, a team of a dozen or so young performers whose athleticism and passion would shame most members of our various and floundering sports franchises. Founded in 1997 by husband and wife Jeffrey Jenkins and Julie Greenberg, the Midnight Circus is a clever concoction that can charm adults and kids.

Jenkins is a former clown with Ringling Bros. and Barnum & Bailey circus, and Greenberg's background is in theater and film. What they have created combines circus and theater in joyful fashion for, as Greenberg likes to say, audiences of "all ages between four and eighty."

Since 1997, the circus has performed at such venues as Theater on the Lake, the bygone Ivanhoe, and the North Shore Center for the Performing Arts. But without a permanent home, the group's performers must rehearse wherever they can, which in one case, has been a vacant lot at the corner of Grand and Wolcott Avenues.

That is where Osgood's camera captured the agile and courageous Amanda Crockett, soaring through the city sky. She and other circus members did this almost every day, weather permitting, during the spring, summer, and fall.

It was one of the great city sights, often causing people driving down the street to stop and get out of their cars.

But some of the neighbors we talked to had become jaded, as if seeing trapeze artists was no more unusual than seeing kids play hopscotch or jump rope.

"They are nice people," said one elderly woman on her way to the grocery store. "And young. You have to be young to do what they do."

They are doing what they do through October 31 in Daley Plaza as part of the city's "Haunted Hijinx 2002" festivities. It's a grueling schedule: five shows a day.

You really should try to catch one. No matter where in the area you live, running away to join the circus is so easy when you've got one in your own backyard.

OCTOBER 27, 2002

AFTER MIDNIGHT OASES

McKinley Park is a Southwest Side neighborhood of hard-working people and at midnight, that hour when much of the city has closed down for the day, the New Archview Restaurant, 3480 South Archer Avenue, is a pleasant and nurturing oasis. The New Archview is part of what I like to think of as a secret city, a Chicago that operates around the clock, a vibrant place in which one can meet the most interesting people.

There's the man in Osgood's photo, for instance. He's one of the New Archview's cooks, as he has been since the place opened twenty-five years ago. But Osgood didn't talk to Emidio Cabada about his expertise with eggs or burgers. Cabada was once a news photographer for *La Voz de la Frontera*, a paper in Mexico, so he and Osgood talked about cameras. One must expect the unexpected in the secret city.

According to the latest statistics from the Department of Labor, nearly 15 percent of full-time wage and salaried employees work hours other than the conventional 9:00 AM to 5:00 PM shift. That represents a lot of people.

They are cops, firefighters, airline workers, cabbies, factory workers, doctors and nurses, and even some newspaper folks.

And if anyone thinks that all the city has to offer them when work ends are some soggy convenience-store sandwiches, check out the action near what's called the "new" Maxwell Street on the city's Near South Side, where you'll find the recently renovated White Palace Grill open all the time.

Hungry for a gyros sandwich at 5:30 AM? Just head over to Greektown Gyros & Ambrosia Sports Bar on South Halsted. Feel like bowling at 7:00 AM or midnight? Try the forty-lane Waveland Bowl at 3700 North Western Avenue or the eighty lanes at Marzano's Miami Bowl, 5032 South Archer Avenue.

In the darkness between midnight and dawn, the city can be a delight.

MARCH 30, 2003

1968 AT FORTY

You might, by the end of this year, be sick and tired of another year: 1968. Already Tom Brokaw has hosted a tame TV special about it, and *Newsweek* gave it a cover. But the first—and what may wind up being the best—trip back took place on the evening of October 13 at the Old Town School of Folk Music: For a couple of amazing hours, that tumultuous year came roaring to life in all its compelling, tuneful, and terrifying complexity.

It came in the form of a show titled *America 1968*, the work of Michael Miles.

A cast of fourteen (not in costume and reading from the script), a live band, and various film images and clips somehow managed to package dozens of events and songs and characters and sights into a show that had the capacity crowd leaping to its feet in a standing ovation.

These are some of the events: Rev. Martin Luther King Jr. and Robert Kennedy are assassinated, the Tet Offensive is launched in Vietnam, Richard Nixon is elected president, the Apollo astronauts visit the dark side of the moon, and the Democratic Convention hits Chicago.

These are some of the songs: "Dance To The Music," "Born To Be Wild," "I Heard It Through The Grapevine," "Jumpin' Jack Flash," "Hey Jude," "Sunshine Of Your Love."

Osgood took pictures—that's John Brennan, as Nixon, in the photo—and I played a small role, reading on stage something that WGN radio's Wally Phillips said in 1968 about the then-ten-year-old Old Town School and how "the five-string banjo takes the place of a five-shot revolver as something [youngsters] want to own, something that will give them an identity."

Miles was fourteen in 1968. Since then he has fashioned a remarkable career in music. A banjo player of international renown, he has made CDs and created all manner of musical/theater shows. *America 1968* is the latest in what he calls his *American Journeys* series and describes as a "mix of imagery, music, pop culture, sound, literature, speeches, letters..."

He could go on, because he started work on *America 1968* four years ago and knows that year as well as anyone. The October performance left Miles "breathless and humbly grateful." The cast, mostly working artist pals of Miles, "was magnificent beyond words," he says.

More than one person in the audience—a nice mix of those not born in 1968 and those who had "make love, not war" bumper stickers on their cars—could not believe that it was a one-time-only performance. "I would go see it again and again," said Shirley Craven, a clinical social worker and ardent theatergoer.

She may get that chance. "I'm hoping to mount it again in Chicago and maybe take a slightly smaller cast on the road to some other venues," says Miles. "I would love to have the time and support to make this happen in a grander way, for a larger audience."

That is what this show deserves: 2008 needs *America 1968*.

JANUARY 6, 2008

TAKE ME TO THE RIVER

Every morning—rain or shine, or, more appropriately for January, snow or wicked wind—the Number 6 Jackson Park Express bus drops me at the southeast corner of Michigan Avenue and Wacker Drive before it turns around to makes its way back south. I, of course, am headed north, because Tribune Tower sits, rather majestically, just across the river. The Michigan Avenue Bridge, built between 1917 and 1920 and 220 feet long, is what gets me there; and every day, no matter the weather, I pause in the middle of that bridge. This is where Chicago comes together for me, in a symphony of buildings and water and sky.

Just a few days before Christmas, a mother and son, he perhaps 12, were on the bridge staring west, and she was saying, "That is where Donald Trump is building his new building," though the kid could have determined that from the ample signage.

The boy nodded his head and pointed his finger at the structure and shouted, "You're fired. You're fired."

Yes, you can see the future from the bridge, but it is also where the past whispers, telling of the Algonquins who found skunk cabbage and wild onion on the banks of the river and affixed to this site the Indian name for those earth products, *Checagou*; of Jean Baptiste Pointe du Sable, the African-American man who became the first nonnative settler here when he built a cabin on the river's northern bank in the 1770s; of the Fort Dearborn massacre of 1812; and of the engineering geniuses who reversed the river's flow in 1900 to keep the lake clean.

Sometimes, I will walk down the stairs and cross the bridge on its lower level, where Osgood took the stunning photo on this page, which always evokes the encounter between Eliot Ness (Kevin Kostner) and cop Jim Malone (Sean Connery) in the 1987 film *The Untouchables*, its screenplay by Chicago's own David Mamet.

In the winter the river is often jammed with ice, and in the summer with boats. The view changes every day, and that, too, is part of the attraction. Maybe you have a special place, a spot in the city that gives you peace and perspective. If not, feel free to share my bridge, my favorite place in my favorite city in the world.

JANUARY 7, 2007

ACKNOWLEDGMENTS

We would like to thank the *Chicago Tribune* which allows us to collaborate with relatively little interference. *Chicago Tribune Magazine* editor Elizabeth Taylor deserves credit for allowing Sidewalks to be born. Jeff Lyon, Marshall Froker, Brenda Butler, Nancy Watkins, and Desiree Chen exercised their expert editorial skills to make each column better than it was when I wrote it. Associate managing editor–photography Torry Bruno has been steady in his support of Osgood's efforts, and magazine photo editor Mike Zajakowski has always made Osgood sweat in the cause of better pictures. David Syrek and Joe Darrow have made the magazine sparkle with their attention to detail and design. Anna Seeto was always on the lookout for Sidewalks subjects. Randy Weissman, deputy managing editor, gently guided us along the newspaper-to-book road. Susan Betz, former editor of Northwestern University Press, came up with the idea of the first book and was its champion.

Without the skills and expertise of our designer and task master, Kim Bartko, the second *Sidewalks* volume, the first to be published by our new company, would never have happened. There are others: Editor Ron Silverman for his keen eye, Julie Anderson for her guidance and feedback, and David Phillips for his brilliant eye and counsel (and scanner). Our families and friends—you know who you are, and we feel fortunate that there are too many of you to mention here—keep us as happy as we are capable of being. Finally, we are most deeply indebted to the people we have met in this ongoing adventure that is Sidewalks, grateful that they allowed us into their lives and let us tell their stories.

ABOUT THE AUTHORS

Born and raised and still living in Chicago, RICK KOGAN has worked for the *Chicago Daily News*, *Chicago Sun-Times*, and the *Chicago Tribune*, where he is currently a senior writer and columnist. A member of the Chicago Journalism Hall of Fame, he is the creator and host of WGN radio's *Sunday Papers with Rick Kogan* and the author of a dozen books, including *Everybody Pays: Two Men, One Murder, and the Price of Truth* (with Maurice Possley); *America's Mom: The Life, Lessons, and Legacy of Ann Landers;* and *A Chicago Tavern*, the history of the Billy Goat.

CHARLES OSGOOD began his career as a reporter for City News Bureau before coming to the *Chicago Tribune* in 1969. After reporting on the south suburbs, and taking photographs to go with the stories, his editor suggested he apply for an opening in the photo department where he might be better suited. He remained there for 38 years. He has also been an adjunct professor of photojournalism at Columbia College since 1991. Osgood left the *Chicago Tribune* in 2008 and continues to pursue his lifelong passion for collecting fleeting moments (and other minutiae). He was born in Milwaukee, Wisconsin, attended Ripon College, and received a master of fine arts in photography from the School of the Art Institute of Chicago.